Getting Heard
The Science and Art of *Effective* Communications

DAVID HILL

Quantity Sales

Most Lakewood Books are available at special quantity discounts when purchased in bulk by companies, organizations and special interest groups. Custom imprinting or excerpting can also be done to fit special needs. For details contact Lakewood Books at (800) 707-7769.

Lakewood Books
50 South Ninth Street
Minneapolis, MN 55402
(800) 328-4329 or (612) 333-0471
(612) 333-6526
http://www.trainingsupersite.com

Publisher: Linda Klemstein
Editor: Paul Nolan
Production Manager: Kimberly Shannon
Production Editor: Ward Barnett, WBCS, Inc.
Proofing: Patty Pryor-Nolan
Illustration: Richard Anderson
Cover Design: Barb Betz, Betz Design
Marketing: Vicki Blomquist

10 9 8 7 6 5 4 3 2 1

Lakewood Publications, Inc. publishes *TRAINING* Magazine, *The Human Side of Business; Training Directors' Forum* Newsletter; *Creative Training Techniques* Newsletter; *Technology for Learning* Newsletter; *Potentials in Marketing* Magazine; Presentations Magazine; and other business periodicals and books. Lakewood also conducts research and develops and presents a variety of conferences.

James P. Secord, president; Mary Hanson, Philip G. Jones, Linda Klemstein, Bryan Powell and Jerry Noack, vice presidents.

ISBN: 0-943210-73-9

Acknowledgments

Publishing is a team sport, and the Getting Heard team sported three all-stars. Paul Nolan edited my thoughts and words with insight and friendship. Dick Anderson illustrated them with wit and charm. And Kim Shannon orchestrated everything with aplomb (as far as I could tell). I'm grateful to them all.

I'm also grateful to a group of people who contributed "between the lines:" the many great clients I've been lucky enough to work with over the years. Clients are the unsung heroes of most communications successes — and all of mine.

Contents

*The greatest problem with communication
is the assumption that it has taken place.*
— George Bernard Shaw

*Think about all the communications that were beamed at you yesterday — via
newspapers, magazines, TV, radio, billboards, direct mail, the Internet, telephone,
slide shows, what have you. How many "took place?"*

*That is, how many did you pay attention to? How many did you act on? How many
do you remember today?*

The ether is filled with communications that haven't "taken place" because they
didn't get heard.

Until someone hears you, you haven't communicated (shades of the tree falling
in the forest). And until someone believes you, you haven't communicated effectively.

This book is about communicating effectively.

A blueprint, not a formula

What's ahead is no "sure-fire formula for success." Rather it's a practical hand-
book, an "owner's manual," that's based on a proven methodology that will dramatically improve your chances of success — and greatly reduce the risk of flops. Your
souffle may not rise as high as you'd hoped, but it will taste good, and it won't give
your guests indigestion.

Why do so many communications go unheard? Too often, it's because their
authors are impatient. They don't take the time to ***plan their approach***. Once you've
read *Getting Heard* this won't happen to you. You'll have a planning methodology —
a blueprint, if you will — that you can use to help create all sorts of communications, from informal foil presentations to colleagues to multimedia ad campaigns to
customers and prospects.

If you're like my students, colleagues and clients, in time this blueprint will
become second nature — something you'll use almost automatically. You'll become
adept at applying it quickly; and your communications will be much likelier to get
heard as a consequence.

And so will you

The blueprint that's at the core of *Getting Heard* took shape in my mind when I
was teaching evening classes in advertising and marketing communications at
Golden Gate University in San Francisco. Once it became clear, I introduced it to
the staff and clients I worked with in my day job. (After 15 years creating advertising

for everything from Razzies cupcakes to mortuary services, I cofounded a corporate communications company and was its chief executive officer and creative director for 16 years.)

As clients began to use the blueprint successfully, an interesting (and thoroughly delightful) thing happened: They won the respect of skeptics in their organizations. They now had something they could hold up to demonstrate that their craft had both method and substance. With luck, this will happen to you, too.

A layered read

The first chapter of *Getting Heard* introduces the blueprint and provides an overview of its components. Then we dive in.

Chapters two through eight focus on the blueprint's fundamental first steps: building a foundation for your communications initiatives*, doing the unglamorous, invisible spade work that will almost certainly pay dividends down the road. These efforts won't guarantee that you'll get heard, but they sure will improve your odds.

Then we'll turn to what I call the "heart of the matter," four chapters that focus on creating compelling, credible, persuasive messages that move audiences to think, feel and act the way you want them to.

The final eight chapters deal with teaming up, message placement (getting the best bang for your buck), message extension (getting more bang for your buck), message and program evaluation, naming and a few tips, tricks and observations.

Chapters two through 15 and chapter 17 begin with executive summaries for those who want only a general understanding of the blueprint's application, or for those who want to get a general sense before digging in.

Following these summaries, we get specific, with how-to's, examples, tips, tricks, anecdotes, war stories, bloopers and pitfalls to avoid. If you're a communications professional, my hunch is you'll find these specifics well worth the time and energy it takes to mine them, if only because they will help you deal more successfully with those who pressure you to take short cuts. ("We have to launch in four weeks! Make some assumptions!")

*The planning methodology, or blueprint, that you will read about in *Getting Heard* lends itself to a wide variety of communications activities — everything from informal presentations to colleagues and one-time speeches to civic groups to ongoing ad campaigns and investor relations programs. The word "initiative," which you will see often as you read on, is a stand-in for this variety.

Chapter 1

The Blueprint

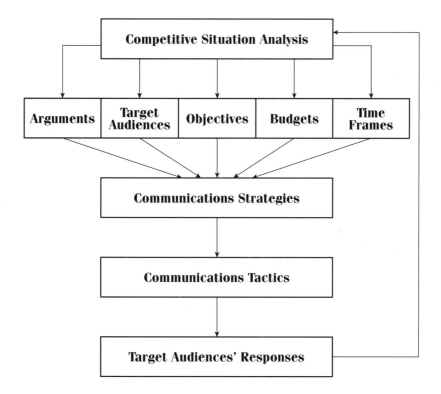

The blueprint you see here consists of four phases: laying the groundwork, pouring the foundation, creating the communication and remodeling the communication as warranted based on audience response.

(I borrow from the language of architects and builders because I believe effective communications are, to a great degree, "architected" and "built." A great communication is much like an elegant building, a combination of thoughtful planning and inspired artistry.)

The essential phase one

To lay the groundwork for a communications initiative, it's essential to define as thoroughly as possible what I call the "situation."

In the case of a speech, the situation consists of the physical environment, the nature of the get-together, the other speakers, their subjects and style, the batting order, the time of day, the composition and interests of the audience and any other contextual component.

If you're creating an ad campaign, a sales promotion, a brochure or a video for a product or service, the situation is the lay of the land in the marketplace.

That is, how is your product or service performing vis-à-vis its rivals? What are its relative strengths and weaknesses? What trends are underway? Are there discernible patterns (regional, seasonal, demographic)? Who's buying? Who's not buying? Why? What are the middlemen — wholesalers, retailers, distributors — up to? How do they see market developments?

Suffice it to say, whether you're delivering a talk to your local Rotary Club or creating a capabilities video for institutional investors, the more you know about the situation, the better your chances of getting heard.

Imagine that you're the captain of a football team. You wouldn't consider leading your players onto the field until you had learned all you could about what they were likely to be up against. You'd understand that the more you were able to find out — the better your intelligence — the greater the likelihood that your team would be successful.

The same holds true when you're creating communications.

Phase two: essential definitions

Once you know the lay of the land, you're ready to pour the foundation. Specifically, you're ready to define your audience(s), argument(s), objective(s), budget (how much it makes sense to invest to achieve your objectives) and time frame (how much time you have to achieve your objective).

Each of these definitions is crucial, and, once again, the more substantial they are, the better your chances of getting heard.

So what constitutes a substantial definition of your audience? First, you need to know how much they know about your subject (product, service, point of view) and how they feel about it vs. its rivals. Then you need to learn as much as you can about them (age, gender, educational backgrounds, professions, vocations, avocations, etc.).

Try to get beyond the superficial. Look for the less visible, more subtle ties that bind. Say, for example, that you're able to determine that nearly everyone in an audience you're speaking to enjoys golf; *voila!* You can use golf metaphors and anecdotes to gain and hold their attention.

Now that you have an understanding of your audience, you're ready to do something most people find exceedingly difficult. You're ready to step outside yourself, empathize with your audience and re-examine your message from their point of view. What is it about what you have to say that your audience is apt to find relevant, interesting and compelling? These are your arguments.

Bear in mind, their interests may not square with yours. You're an expert on your subject. You have your own views about what makes it fascinating. But they don't count or, at least, they're secondary. And you have to be prepared to jettison them or rearrange them. What matters — if you're really interested in getting heard — is what it is about your offering that your audience cares about.

Now what is it that you want your communications initiative to accomplish? Over what time frame? How do you want your audience to think, feel or act after they've heard you? How long after they've heard you?

Be specific. Do you want X percent to call a toll-free number within 24 hours? Y percent to give you their business cards before they leave the room? Z percent to take the call when one of your sales reps telephones? Are you simply looking to reinforce your already stellar reputation, or are you desperately trying to avoid Chapter 11 at the 11th hour?

Defining your objectives in measurable terms such as these will not only help you shape your communication, it will also enable you to know — and to show others — objectively how well you did.

And it will enable you to determine more intelligently how much to invest in your presentation. Suppose you prompted 100 members of your audience to call a toll-free number within 24 hours. Translate that into dollars and cents. Then you can calculate how much it makes sense to invest in your communications initiative. You can come up with a legitimate, zero-based budget.

That should make your chief financial officer happy.

To borrow again from the language of construction, now that you've set your definitions (or cornerstones, as I call them), you've effectively poured the foundation. Obviously, the better the definitions, the stronger the foundation.

You're almost ready to get creative, but not quite.

The fifth definition

For a communications initiative to stand on a truly solid foundation, one final definition is required. You have to gain a thorough understanding of the individual, group or organization you're communicating *for* so your communication will accurately reflect their character. An effective communication not only connects with its audience, it conveys the identity and personality of its sponsor.

Time to get creative

You've prepared the ground (the situation) and you've set the foundation, or cornerstones. Five of them. You understand the target audience and the arguments you can advance that will appeal to them. You've defined a measurable objective and set a time frame for achieving it. And you've determined how much money you can afford to invest to achieve it.

Now all you have to do to get heard is to communicate the relevant information to your audience in a way that prompts them to think/feel/act as you or your sponsor wants them to…within your budget and time frame.

What could be simpler?

Lots. Straightforward is not simple. Your task now is to find ways to make the information come to life for your audience. Make it compelling, fascinating, exciting, riveting, irresistible — not to mention credible and persuasive. You have to turn a set of words on a piece of paper into something dramatic, something that so involves your audience that — as skeptical, distracted and time-constrained as they are — they can't not pay attention.

That's no small challenge. Just think how seldom you're on the receiving end of communications that you feel compelled to pay attention to.

We'll tackle this challenge in detail in chapter nine. For now, here's an overview of how to meet it: Use your powers of free association. Use them to find ways to connect with your audience on an emotional level, human being to human being.

Use metaphors, analogies, humor, color and sound. Tell stories — personal stories. Pose rhetorical questions and non-rhetorical questions. Engage your audience in a dialogue.

You can do it

Everyone can. The oft-heard excuse "I'm not creative" just isn't true. Everyone is creative in his or her own way. Some are more artistic than others, to be sure, just as some are less inhibited. But we all have the capacity to interest others. It's inside us. We simply need to sit back, relax and take however long it takes to access it. Creativity can't be hurried. Quite the opposite. The more pressure you put on yourself, the harder it is to access your creative capability.

Hence, the free association approach, where you mull over the points you want to make, letting them percolate until, at some unexpected moment, when you're in the shower or driving your car, ideas start popping, seemingly unbidden, to mind.

Say you want to make the point that your company has 12 applications engineers. What does the number 12 call to mind? A dozen roses? The number of hours on a clock? Two six-fingered hands? The square root of 144? An X and two Is? Which of these associations is your audience especially likely to relate to? Maybe they're sports car enthusiasts. If so, you might want to compare the number of applications engineers at your company to the number of cylinders in a Ferrari racing engine.

The medium

At the same time you're concocting a strategy for expressing your message, you should be thinking about what media vehicles you'll use to deliver it. In fact, these two considerations should go hand in hand. Your choice of a medium for your communication may dictate — and will certainly influence — how you dramatize it.

If your communications initiative is a speech or presentation, your media vehicle is predetermined: You're it. What you need to think about are the audio and visual aids you can conceivably employ to energize your message.

If, on the other hand, you're working on a program that will rely on one or another of "the media" to deliver your messages, you'll find it helpful to apply a few selection criteria.

Selection criteria

There are five things to think about when you're evaluating the various media vehicles. The first is **affordability**. If you have a modest four- or five-figure budget, prime-time television is not a candidate.

The second is **reach** or **coverage**. You want to make sure that the media vehicles you choose reach all, or nearly all, of your target audience.

The third consideration, **frequency**, is particularly critical given that we live in a time when nearly all of us are deluged with information — the Information Overload Age, I call it. Simply put, you want to be sure that no matter what media vehicles you choose, you're able to use them often enough to get your message to your audience repeatedly.

Unless your message and its presentation are exceptionally dramatic ("You don't have to worry about cancer anymore!"), it will take repetition to drive it home to your audience.

6

Now let's say that you've made a list of all the media vehicles that cover your audience and that you can afford to use often. (How often? See chapter 14.) Now you're ready to think about **efficiency**, or cost per target audience member delivered.

As you know, when you buy space or time from a medium, the price you pay is based on its total audience, so if your audience consists only of nuclear physicists, you want a media vehicle whose audience consists largely of nuclear physicists. Think target audience per dollar. That's efficiency.

The fifth consideration is **context**. That is, how well does the medium fit your message? If visuals are an integral part of it, you probably won't use radio. (Although, used adroitly, radio can create wonderful images in listeners' minds. Stan Freberg, a master at using sounds to create pictures, has long argued that radio is the best visual medium. If you're old enough to have listened to radio programs such as "Suspense," "Lights Out" and "Inner Sanctum," you know what he means.)

Another aspect of context is the medium's editorial subject matter. If your message pertains to vacation travel, for example, you'll want to take a good look at media that focus on leisure travel, even if they're less efficient than other, more general media vehicles.

Cooking in the shower

Your head is now fully loaded. You're thinking simultaneously about how to dramatize your message and where to place it. Things are percolating. Which means you're a prime candidate for shower-time revelations.

You know what to do. Empathize with your target audience, take a couple of deep breaths, revisit your five cornerstones and start free associating. Inspiration — in the form of communications strategies — will strike in good time. I guarantee it.

You say you're stuck? Try "B.S.ing."

You've heard about "writer's block." In fact, you've probably experienced it. It's the sedentary equivalent of an athlete's slump, and it's not only extremely frustrating, it's also one of those awful maladies that gets worse the longer it persists. Those of us who aim to create effective communications are especially susceptible.

So what are we to do? Find a knowledgeable friend or colleague or two and brainstorm (a.k.a. "B.S."). That is, free-associate together. We'll explore the dos and don'ts of brainstorming in detail in chapter nine. For now, suffice it to say there are two keys to successful brainstorming: trust and a shared understanding that there's no such thing as a stupid idea.

If you and I are to brainstorm successfully together, we both have to be able to say whatever comes to mind, spontaneous and unrehearsed, without precensoring. We'll only be able to do this if we both understand that everything that's said is, by definition, valuable.

Why? Because something I say, regardless of how ridiculous or seemingly irrelevant it might appear, might — just might — prompt you to come up (and out) with something absolutely brilliant. Of such insights are mega-millionaires made.

Getting Heard

What to say when they say, "Guess!"

When you're pressured to take short cuts, start by reminding your adversaries of the stakes: A communications flop is more than a waste of money; it's also a signal to your audiences that you've lost your way.

If this doesn't take the heat off you, drop football commentator John Madden's name. Point out just how conspicuously successful he has become simply by taking the time and energy to do his homework — to carefully plan and build a foundation for his communications that's as rock solid as Bronco Nagurski.

(You say you're being pressured by people who've never heard of John Madden, much less Bronco Nagurski? Then reference conspicuously effective communicators from other fields — journalists Cokie Roberts and David Halberstam, authors Tom Clancy and Patricia Cornwell, or scholars Barbara Tuchman and David McCollough.)

Still being pressured? Propose a compromise: Use the blueprint to build a scaled-down "bridge" initiative, based on "best guesses," to be implemented on an interim basis while you're completing the requisite knowledge-based foundation.

Just make sure you scale down expectations along with everything else.

Tactics

You've been visited by inspiration. Your muse has responded. You've conceived a solid set of communications strategies. Now it's time to get specific. To return again to the builder's idiom, it's time to buy the materials — the boards, nails, concrete and glass — and start putting them in place.

Say you've decided to use the Ferrari racing engine metaphor — an appropriate strategy. How are you going to use it? Will you go to a sound effects library and buy a recording of a Ferrari at LeMans? Will you marry it to a series of still photos of Ferraris in action? Or to photos of your applications engineers?

Or maybe you'll decide to lift a two-minute segment from the classic film "Grand Prix" (check with your lawyers first), or to pay a visit to your neighborhood Ferrari dealer to see what sorts of props he might be able to give you.

When we talk about tactics in the context of a communications initiative, we're talking about collecting and assembling the elements we'll use to turn our brilliant strategies into compelling messages.

Feedback

Not only are we living in the Information Overload Age, we also are living in the Interactivity Age. Our world is filled with mechanisms that enable us to respond to communications we receive, to engage our correspondents in ongoing dialogues, no matter where they happen to be. Technologies have redefined distance and time.

This is a boon to communicators because it provides us with unprecedented opportunities to learn from our target audiences. Today, we can virtually place our fingers on our audiences' collective pulse and almost instantly monitor their reactions to our initiatives.

This means we can fine-tune them as warranted, midstream, as it were. Equally important, we can use feedback to update and sharpen our situation analysis and close the blueprint's loop.

Commandments

One day an authoritarian client decided that he could improve upon my blueprint by turning it into what he called "The Five Commandments," which he then published in poster form and distributed to his staff. Here, for those who resonate more with directives than diagrams, is what he wrote:

- Know the situation.
- Know who you're talking to.
- Know what you're talking about.
- Know what you're trying to achieve…and how much time and money you have to achieve it.
- Know who you're talking for.

So what does it mean, really, to "know the situation?" Good question. See chapter two for answers.

Chapter 2

What's Going On Out There?

Executive Summary

Objectives:

(1) Gain a clear and complete view of marketplace realities (e.g., shifts in attitudes and buying patterns, trends) from the user's, buyer's, influencer's, seller's, middleman's and industry analyst's perspective.

(2) Learn how all of your offering's potential users, buyers and purchase influencers regard it relative to its competitors.

Strategies:

(1) Listen. Interview the people who use, buy, influence, study, sell, distribute and make your offering.

(2) Read. Collect and analyze information published about your and rivals' offerings by their producers, industry analysts and the trade press.

(3) Collect and analyze information about your offering's potential users, buyers and influencers — from media vehicles, government agencies, trade associations, colleges and universities, elected representatives and employees.

(4) Consider buying research data. Evaluate data generated and sold by research companies as well as possible participation in multi-sponsor surveys conducted by these companies.

(5) Commission proprietary research. Surveys designed and conducted expressly for you by independent polling firms.

The ideal:

A combination of one, two and five. Read everything you can that's germane. Interview everyone you can who's germane. Commission an in-depth survey of a representative sample of potential users, buyers and influencers. Then mix and match for a revelatory situation analysis.

"I'm reviewing the sit…u…a…tion."

Remember the villainous Fagin in Charles Dickens' *Oliver?* Ultimately (and happily), he's trapped by his self-centered view of things. Only in defeat does he realize this and lament that it's time to "review the situation."

Like Fagin, we're all prisoners of perspective. What we think depends on what we see. So it's important, nay essential, to get a clear view of marketplace realities if we're serious about getting heard by the people who frequent this marketplace.

And we can't trust our colleagues and clients to do this for us. Not because they're untrustworthy, but because, to mix metaphors, the folks on the 40th floor typically wear rose-colored glasses.

They tend to see only what they want to see — or what their lieutenants want them to see.

So we must venture forth, out of our offices and into the marketplace, make like investigative reporters and wander around, ever alert.

For what?

Short answer: How does the offering we'll be communicating about compare with its rivals *in the eyes of* current and prospective users, buyers and influencers? What do they see as its strengths and weaknesses? How have their views changed over time?

What matters are users', buyers' and influencers' perceptions, no matter how wildly inaccurate they may be. As communicators, our reality is what they think and feel.

Note that buyers are often different from users (e.g., parents buy but rarely use Cocoa Puffs) and that, for every buyer, there may be four or five influencers (e.g., when it comes to buying a new family car, Mr. and Mrs. will consult with each other, with friends, with professional advisers, with published guides, etc.).

This is especially true in the business marketplace. For example, computers that are used by a company's administrative assistants are bought by a purchasing agent after evaluations by his/her staff, consultations with the chief information officer and his/her staff and approvals from administration and finance department heads…with a couple of committee rubber stamps for good measure.

All of which is to say, getting a fix on the views of users, buyers and influencers is a big job.

But what if your assignment is to communicate to investors about a company's stock, or to employees about its health plan, or to opinion leaders about its environmental programs? The approach is the same. Just substitute "investors," "employees" or "opinion leaders" for "users and buyers."

And note that you'll still have "influencers" to understand — securities analysts, family doctors, environmental writers and the like.

Don't ignore makers and sellers

The people who design, engineer, manufacture, market and sell your offering have a bias, to be sure, but this doesn't for a minute mean that they don't have valuable points of view about what's happening in the marketplace and why. Seek out these men and women, and listen carefully — and critically — to what they say.

By the numbers?

If you have ever worked for a consumer products outfit, you know just how complex, comprehensive and statistical their market situation analyses tend to be. Printouts by the ream.

How important is it for communicators to familiarize themselves with these data? I think it's important to pay attention to them — and to the people who produce them — only insofar as they'll help you get a better fix on how users, buyers and influencers see your subject. Mastering the intricacies of shipment volumes probably won't help you create a more effective A/V presentation, brochure or ad campaign.

It's buyers', influencers' and users' views that matter to you, but you'll often find useful clues about these views either in a printout or among the interpretations of the analysts responsible for it.

Attention! Paradox ahead!

Beware. It's possible to spend so much time studying the situation that it will have changed by the time you're finished.

I recall a project that called for a complicated computer analysis of an area's weather patterns. There were so many variables — and they changed so often — that the project manager wasn't sure he could find a computer fast enough to do the job.

Market situations, like the weather, change often (in fact, constantly). What you're out to do is to take a snapshot of your market at a given point in time…and act on it before it becomes outdated.

Another fact of life that will probably prevent you from dallying too long on your situation analysis: the deadline for your communications initiative.

Another set of eyes and ears

In your quest to learn how buyers, influencers and users see your offering relative to its rivals, you may have a couple of resources that communicators often overlook: middlemen (and middlewomen) and industry gurus.

The wholesalers, distributors, dealers, agents and retailers who handle your offering and the independent analysts who evaluate and write about it typically have terrific perspectives on users, buyers and influencers — in part because they tend to be no-nonsense and clear-eyed, and in part because they collect all sorts of anecdotal and "off-the-record" information in the course of doing their jobs.

Getting answers 1-2-3-4

The objective is straightforward: Find out how current and prospective users, buyers and influencers see your offering vis-à-vis its rivals. The question is how.

There are four general ways to get answers: Conduct interviews, collect and analyze published information, purchase proprietary research, commission original research. All are useful; the first is essential.

Nothing is as enlightening as watching and listening to the people who make, distribute, sell, study, use and buy your offering. Get out from behind your desk or drawing board and get with them — face to face if possible. (Eighty percent of all communication is lost when it takes place via telephone.)

If you do this consistently, in time you'll create a network of great sources, much as a journalist (or an intelligence agent) does. A network like this is extraordinarily useful, especially when you're confronted with tight deadlines. It should be nurtured and carefully maintained.

A friend's dad was a long-time sports columnist for a Boston newspaper. He worked diligently to nurture and maintain what he called his "morning after" sources — people he could count on for a good story when he was hung over and "on deadline." They served him well for many years.

Teetotalers, too, can learn from his experience.

The art of interviewing

Surprise! Interviewing users, buyers, influencers and middlepeople is not at all like the interviews you see on television news programs.

First of all, there's nothing adversarial about these interviews. Your objective is to learn from your interviewees, not trap them in contradictions. You're talking *with*, not to, or at. You and the person you're interviewing are engaged in a joint exploration, an inquiry, not a debate. And your job is to listen hard and prompt gently. To draw out.

Your job is not to impress your subjects with your knowledge, wisdom, charm and wit. Keep your views and insights to yourself.

Second, there's a lot less time pressure. Ideally, you and your subjects will spend enough time together to allow for a relaxed, informal, unhurried conversation. You'll be able to set your interviewees at ease, have an exchange that's spontaneous and unrehearsed, so you can pick up on asides and "oh, by the ways." Answers should be seen as grist for subsequent questions. Nothing is irrelevant. A side track may lead to a gold mine.

It takes time for people to get over their self-consciousness. And you can't hurry them. In fact, your job is to attune yourself to their pace and then adopt it. We all tend to get a little tongue-tied (or tight-lipped) when we're put on the spot. And so we tighten up or slow down. The artistic interviewer understands this.

Artistic interviewers also understand that the timing and location of an interview will make a big difference in its quality. Offices and conference rooms tend to be terrible places to conduct interviews. Eateries aren't much better — too many distractions. The best time and place, by definition, is when and where the interviewee feels most comfortable — an evening in his or her study, Saturday morning at a picnic table on the back lawn.

One of my key sources is his company's chief executive officer, ergo, much in demand at all times. His solution is to take me for noontime walks. We stroll along and he reflects and ruminates and pats himself on the back for forgoing lunch. There's only one drawback: It's hell taking notes.

(Luddite that I am, I don't like tape recorders. They intrude, and the tape always runs out at the worst possible moment. Murphy's Law in action.)

I once interviewed the head of product development for a mainframe computer company, a brilliant design engineer, and I couldn't get him to tell me anything about his creations that wasn't in the data sheets. Finally, it occurred to me: Change the venue. We moved our conversation from an executive conference room to his test lab, sat on the floor in front of one of his "babies" minus its shell, and had one of the most animated, enlightening conversations I've ever participated in.

Rule of thumb: Be sensitive to your interviewees; meet when and where they want for as long as they want; let them set the pace.

CBS distinguished itself in the 1970s when it broadcast each year an hour-long "Conversation with Walter Lippmann." The CBS correspondent, usually Eric Sevareid, would guide the famous pundit on a tour through the issues of the day with no more than a quick question here and an interjection there. The guiding was so subtle that viewers were largely unaware of it. We heard what we tuned in to hear: Lippmann's views and ideas.

Today, two interviewers stand out as especially artistic: Terri Gross of National Public Radio's "Fresh Air" and Bill Moyers. Both have the wonderful ability to make their guests feel important. They seem to hang on their guests' every word. And they give their guests and their audiences the sense that they have no agenda, that they're simply following their subjects' leads.

They're also good at probing sensitive areas in a nonthreatening way. ("Some people say…I think you deserve a chance to respond…"). Gross once asked Audrey Hepburn how she felt about being flat-chested, and her question was so sympathetically phrased that Hepburn, far from being offended, launched into a long and touching discourse on the topic.

As important, both Gross and Moyers resist the temptation to do the one thing that's sure to foul up an interview: interrupt. You, too, will be tempted, especially when your interviewee meanders off point. Resist! Hold your tongue! To interrupt your interviewees is to say to them that you aren't really listening and aren't really interested in what they have to say.

What's more, what seem at the outset to be meanderings usually turn out to be unconventional ways to make important points.

The sounds of silence

Silence may be golden, but it's also discomfiting. The temptation when you're interviewing someone is to end it with another question or an aside. Don't. Let the person you're interviewing end it. Pauses, even long ones, can lead to valuable elaborations or revelations.

Listening between the lines

Obviously, I'm partial to personal, face-to-face interviews as a way to understand how users, buyers and influencers see the offering I'm supposed to communicate about; but, in fairness, I should acknowledge a contrary viewpoint.

There are those who maintain that talking with these people is a waste of time because they can't tell you how they really feel about product X, service Y or candidate Z. Why not? Because their real feelings are inchoate, virtually inexpressible and often largely unconscious. Hence, the only way to learn how people really feel is to observe their behavior; employ the techniques of social science.

I'm all for observation, though it's often not very practical when it comes to situation analyses, but I'm for conversations, too, for two reasons: First, I believe most people are quite capable of telling you a lot about how they think and feel about a product, service or candidate; and, second, I believe if you listen carefully ("between the lines") you can pick up attitudes they may not be able to articulate.

Double-backs

Pollsters frequently reinterview a sample or a portion of a sample after a few weeks or months to help them measure opinion shifts. They call these reinterviews "double-backs."

I find that this is a good thing to do when you're trying to understand marketplace realities. Revisit your key sources from time to time, not only to see whether and to what degree their views have changed, but to get their reactions to your views. They can help you see better.

Bearding the opposition

When you're out interviewing, there's a natural tendency to steer clear of people who hold negative views of your subject. Don't. The skeptical environmental activist, the cynical industry guru and the unsympathetic editor are terrific resources. Just remember that your job is not to debate them, but rather to put them at ease, draw them out and learn why they feel as they do. You'll have stimulating conversations.

I once interviewed a man who was a trade union's chief lobbyist in a midwestern state capital. He had little use for the service my client offered and agreed to be interviewed most reluctantly. He was ill at ease and his comments were mostly boilerplate. Then I discovered that he was a former Jesuit priest. I mentioned that I had been educated by Jesuits. And his reluctance melted immediately. We swapped funny stories, had a fine time and I learned a lot about an influential group.

One-on-one

When you're interviewing users, buyers and influencers, is it better to talk with them individually or in groups? Given the choice, I almost always opt for one-on-one sessions. Generally, people tend to be more comfortable when there are no "witnesses."

People who care about confidentiality — and who doesn't? — can preserve deniability when they're interviewed one-on-one. If you leak, they deny, and it's your word against theirs. Managers also tend to be more comfortable when there are no subordinates to impress. And people who are laconic or shy tend to do better when they don't have anyone to defer to.

The scene: the board room of a large manufacturing company. Across a massive oak table sit the CEO and the COO, a pair of no-nonsense manufacturing types who had worked together forever.

My mission: loosen their tongues, induce them to hold forth about the company and its customers and prospects. I failed.

The CEO never answered a question, even when I addressed him directly by name. He just sat there, stone-faced, while his COO did the talking. I could only assume that what I heard from his surrogate (mouthpiece?) represented his views.

When we came to know one another better, they acknowledged with smiles that they developed this routine years earlier as a way of dealing with pesky journalists and analysts. It enabled them to take their interviewer's measure first and then decide how much to divulge.

Moral: Don't let your interviewees double up on you if you can avoid it.

Reading

The second way to get good situation data is to get your hands on everything you can that has been written about your subject and its rivals. Articles in the trade press. Releases from competitors and industry associations. Web sites. Congressional testimony. White papers authored by industry gurus, academics and their graduate students.

Lexis-Nexis. The Internet. Your elected representatives. Government agencies. Trade groups. Foundations. Institutes. Trade and consumer books, magazines, newspapers and newsletters. The sources are almost endless. So you should have no trouble compiling a bibliography that will keep you behind your desk with your specs on for six months.

The trick, of course, is to separate the wheat from the chaff, and, here again, the people you interview can help. Ask them what they read and what they recommend that you read. You can also help yourself by remembering what you are — and are not — looking for: information about how current and prospective users, buyers and influencers see your offering vs. its rivals. If it won't shed light on their views, don't read it.

Buying research

As you know, there are companies that sell market data (e.g., A. C. Nielsen) and that field discounted, multi-sponsor, "omnibus" surveys you can buy a share of (e.g., Opinion Research Corp). What about these as situation information sources?

Only if you're desperate. The data you get from the Nielsens of this world probably won't tell you a whole lot about current and prospective users', buyers' and influencers' attitudes toward your offering. And omnibus surveys don't give you a chance to shape the sample or ask an extended series of questions.

In general, I urge my clients to put the money they would have spent on a share of an omnibus survey toward designing and fielding their own custom-tailored survey of their particular audiences.

Original research

The next best thing to "being there," and a good complement to being there. A well-designed telephone survey of users, buyers and influencers will deliver valuable situation data quickly and economically.

Just make sure the samples are large enough to allow you to draw statistically significant conclusions and that the questions are written by a professional researcher who knows what she or he is doing. Ask the right question the wrong way, and what you get back is worse than useless, it's poisonous.

Questionnaire writing, like interviewing, is an art. Don't entrust the task to anyone who isn't demonstrably good at it.

How about group discussions (focus groups)? Useful if used correctly. (See chapter eight.) Generally, focus groups are more helpful later in the process, when it's time to concoct imaginative ways to say what you want to say.

I've had good luck using focus groups to help me collect situation data when I'm dealing with a small, well-defined marketplace (a company's employees, for example).

A client asked my company to create an ongoing communications program whose objective was to instill pride and spirit in his company's work force. We began by holding group discussions that brought together employees from different departments, and we opened these discussions by asking the participants to complete a questionnaire. This enabled us to get their individual views before they were "tainted" by others in their groups.

What if?

What if the offering you're charged with communicating about is a new kind of product or service, an offering the likes of which no one has seen before, a la Sony's Walkman or 3M's Post-it Notes? How can you determine prospective users', buyers' and influencers' attitudes toward it?

You can't. What you can do is to determine their attitudes toward the product or service it aims to replace, or to the unmet want or need it aims to fill.

Let's say your new product is an auxiliary motor for mountain bikes. Its function is to assist mountain bikers when they're negotiating particularly steep climbs, when they're tired and when they're in a hurry.

You'd talk with a variety of mountain bikers about the concept of "power assistance," the possible applications of it, their attitudes toward it and how much they imagine they'd pay for it. And you'd come away with a good sense of the marketplace realities.

The ideal

Let's suppose your client or boss says you can have all the time and money you want to do your communications situation analysis. How much and how long should it take?

Remember the objective: find out how current and prospective users, buyers and influencers see the offering you'll be communicating about vis-à-vis its rivals…in depth.

What will it take to accomplish this? A combination of reading (for background), surveying (for breadth) and interviewing (for depth).

Start by compiling two lists: a bibliography and a list of the people you'd like to interview. Asterisk the people you'd like to reinterview.

Then start talking with research firms — at least three. Explain that you want to survey a representative sample of current and prospective users, buyers and influencers, and ask them how they'd approach the assignment, how long they think it would take and how much they think it would cost.

Check their references; select one; develop a questionnaire; pilot test it; then field the survey. It will probably take six to eight weeks to complete.

Concurrently, spend one of those weeks reading and five to seven interviewing. Do not use a questionnaire. Talking points are fine; a questionnaire will get in your way and inhibit spontaneity.

By the time the survey results arrive, you'll be ready to integrate them into the conclusions you've gained from your reading and interviewing. Give yourself a week to complete this integration.

Your report should be both concise and profound. A dozen points that capture, in depth and detail, current and prospective users', buyers' and influencers' attitudes toward your offering vis-à-vis rivals.

Cost? Hard to say. The big variables are the cost of the survey and the cost of your time. Best guess: between $35,000 and $100,000.

Time? Nine to 12 weeks.

Sound expensive? It isn't. Not when you consider the applications of the situation analysis beyond your communications initiative.

It will also help in sales, marketing and distribution. And remember, once you've done it, you can do it again, in a year or two, for considerably less.

Hidden in plain sight

Speaking of doing it again, here's a paradox: The best situation analyses are those that are designed to be forever unfinished. They employ methods that generate timely market intelligence on an ongoing basis, much as a doctor uses medical devices to continuously monitor an unstable patient.

The best of these methods has until recently been ignored, or dismissed, by all but a few marketers despite its obviousness. I proposed it to a client company in 1992 and found that I couldn't get its market research people to put it in place, despite their president's enthusiastic endorsement.

Why? Another paradox. The method I proposed promised to produce intelligence that too many people could benefit from. The heads of three departments — marketing, product development and corporate research and development — all wanted to control it, but each insisted that the others help fund it.

Many other companies also have found this turf obstacle to be insurmountable, but according to a recent article in *Business Week*, some are finding ways around it. They're beginning to appreciate its extraordinary value, and they've figured out that they'll be at a disadvantage if they don't use it and their rivals do.

You'll understand the method as soon as I tell you what I call it. First, let me lift a quote from *Business Week*'s article to underscore its value. An executive observed, "Eighty percent of what we need to know is inside our company."

Grapevines and gossip czars, for super situation analyses

"The grapevine." You've heard the term for years in connection with prisons, right? An invisible, ethereal, super-efficient intranet. A network of drums without the drums, silent but magically effective when it comes to "spreading the word," especially when the "word" wasn't meant to be spread.

My hunch is, there's a grapevine in your organization, and it's no less efficient and effective than the grapevines inside Sing Sing, San Quentin or old Edward G. Robinson/James Cagney movies. What's more important, you and your colleagues know how to access it. No HR maven clued you in when you joined. The password didn't appear in any operations manual. But you learned it nonetheless.

And now you and your marketing, product development and R&D colleagues may be failing to take full advantage of it.

Grapevines, of course, offer two opportunities: the opportunity to communicate to colleagues; and the opportunity to learn from them. It's the latter that I'll focus on.

The CIA in Neverwonderland

Let's suppose for the moment that you are the CIA's top banana in the nation of Neverwonderland. You have agents throughout the country, who, in turn, have sources throughout their areas, with cut-outs, drop-off points, techno-gadgets and secret codes.

It's all very exciting, and, if you were to map it (which you never would, right?), it would look like a tightly woven fishnet that blanketed Neverwonderland, covered all its nooks and crannies.

You, in your turn, would be part of a larger fishnet that covered a region, which would be part of a still larger fishnet that spanned the globe. At least, in theory.

Do you see where I'm going with this? Thanks to its grapevine, your organization already has fishnets in place. The infrastructure is there, waiting to be used to collect information about what's going on in your markets — information that can be analyzed and turned into intelligence policymakers will find invaluable.

So far so good. But...

There are questions. First, do your employees possess enough useful information about your markets to make it worthwhile to collect it? Second, assuming at least some do, how do you get them to pass it on? Third, whom do they pass it on to? Fourth, how do you separate the wheat from the chaff, make sense of what they pass on, evaluate its timeliness and accuracy (especially given that competitors wil! try to infiltrate and ply you with disinformation)? And, fifth, how do you apply what you learn in ways that boost your organization's performance?

(I'm reminded of a baseball oddity: batters who don't want to know what the pitcher is about to throw them, even when a teammate has stolen the opposing catcher's sign. They'd rather guess. Here's hoping you don't have teammates like them.)

Let's tackle the five questions, then we'll look at a prototypical system that collects and analyzes information from a variety of sources, including the grapevine, and produces intelligence for people who need it to make decisions.

Do your employees have useful information?

You bet. Your employees spend time with customers and prospects. They cross paths with suppliers, rivals, journalists and industry gurus, often informally or in social settings. And they hear tidbits. "Did you hear that Joan Jones is changing jobs?" "Joe tells me they're havin' a hell of a time with their new machine." Mix and match tidbits, and you have potential bonanzas.

How do you get them to pass it on?

This is a toughy, because employees' interests often don't coincide with the organization's. Joan Jones might prefer to share her tidbits with her supervisor, or a pal in another department, for political reasons or because she feels that it's more likely to get acted on and redound to her credit. And she may be right.

There are two ways to deal with this. You can hope Joan's boss or pal will pass on what she tells them. Or you can provide incentives that will make it more likely that Joan, boss and pal will all conclude that it's in their interest to pass on what they learn.

Incentives can range from free lunches to a chance at something grand and glorious, like an extra week's vacation or the use of the Concorde for a weekend (or a tank of jet fuel, whichever runs out first). The important thing is that the incentive have real value in the employees' eyes.

Also important: feedback that demonstrates the procedure's value to employees.

Whom do they pass it on to?

Enter the "gossip czar." The gossip czar can be a person, a group or simply a drop-off point. An organization may have one or a bunch (district, regional, national, etc.). The gossip czar's reasons for being are two: (1) to demonstrate that the organization values and acts on its employees' input; and (2) to provide employees a single, secure person/place to deposit their input, an outsized suggestion box, if you will.

Naturally, some organizations will prefer to give their gossip czars a less irreverent title. Fine. Just make sure it clearly describes the function. Also, make sure the gossip czar acknowledges all contributions. It's essential to let people know they've been heard.

How do you separate the wheat from the chaff?

The most immediate objection to a grapevine/gossip czar strategy is: "We'll be flooded, deluged with information, and we'll drown."

The response: You'll be surprised. People, generally, and the people in your organization, particularly, are smart and sensible (not to mention busy), and they're not going to spend their time passing on information unless they think it'll be useful. Chances are, you'll receive less than you expect. But if you're nervous, here's an idea that precludes floods and deluges: Test the notion at one location or in one business unit or region. Then roll it out if/as warranted.

It's certainly true, though, that some of what you receive won't be relevant and that some will have relevance that's hard to pin down. So it's important to set up a system to review and cross-check.

How do you apply what you learn?

Someone in your organization has to take responsibility for combing through haystacks of information and finding needles. This entails setting up an information-gathering and processing system that yields insightful distillations. Best case, your system delivers weekly digests to your organization's policymakers and responds rapidly to questions and directives from them.

It puts the pictures on your president's desk. From then on, it's up to him/her and his/her advisers to formulate effective policies.

A prototypical system

Imagine three information streams that empty into a single pool. The first consists of formal market research (e.g., surveys, focus groups). The second consists of informal or anecdotal market research (e.g., meetings with customers and prospects, store checks, media clips). Number three is the company grapevine.

The pool is the domain of an analytical team whose members compare, contrast, cross-check, interpret, evaluate and report. Their reports go to policymakers in marketing, product development, R&D, sales and general management.

In my prototype, the analytical team is headed by a veteran market researcher who reports to the organization's senior marketing executive. The team's reports resemble *The Kiplinger Letter*: terse, telegraphic, no frou-frou.

How about security?

How does one keep the system from leaking? How does one keep pearls and nuggets from falling into the wrong hands, especially in our two-career age where spouses sometimes work for rivals, suppliers or related outfits? And how does one spot disinformation?

The answer to these questions is another question: How do you keep these things from happening now? What do you do now to secure a market research survey or a sales report? Remember, we're not adding anything new here, just harnessing something that already exists — your organization's grapevine. So the same security techniques that you now use to protect your outfit's information and communications should suffice.

With respect to spotting (and exploiting!) disinformation, that's the analytical team's responsibility. If they're on the ball, they'll see it — or at least have their suspicions aroused — in the course of cross-checking.

Getting started

Harnessing grapevines is tricky. Do it wrong, and you'll create another grapevine. Doing it right means having the CEO or COO own it, having every employee clear about its objective (market insights that will boost the organization's performance and all interested parties' compensation) and providing regular evidence that it's working.

It's also important to make sure employees understand what it's not: a way to collect information about them. Everyone must understand that no one has any interest in learning anything about what's going on inside the organization. Only information about what's going on in the marketplace counts.

Finally, employees should see grapevine and gossip czar as parts of a comprehensive info-gathering, intelligence-producing *system*.

An added benefit

An integrated system like this does more than produce valuable insights. It also illuminates gaps and points up things you don't know and should, so it's much easier to focus and get support for market research initiatives — which, of course, will be much more cost-effective thanks to their sharper focus.

Is it worth it?

That's a question only you can answer. But as you think about it, recall the times that intelligence has helped you and the lack of it has hurt you. Recall also the extraordinary role that intelligence-gathering mechanisms have played in recent U.S. history. The U2. The SR-71 Blackbird. Satellites. Yes, they've been (and are) expensive. But they've yielded a solid gold ROI. They've not only kept us out of trouble, they've helped us cope more effectively when we couldn't avoid it.

Just ask Presidents Ford, Carter, Reagan, Bush and Clinton.

Meanwhile, the question is: How do you use your situation analysis, with all the intelligence you've been able to build into it, to define your communications initiative's cornerstones? The answer is what the next five chapters are all about.

The best I ever saw

Here's one illustration of what a telephone survey can give you:

A company with two arch-rivals fielded a telephone survey of prospects (people it was not currently doing business with who purchased the kinds of products it offered) that asked them to do three things:

- identify their four most important purchase criteria
- rank the importance of each on a 1-10 scale
- rate three suppliers (the study's sponsor and its two arch-rivals) according to these criteria, also on a 1-10 scale

Visualize what this produced (see chart):

- relevant buying criteria with their relative importance quantified
- a profile of the ideal supplier
- profiles of the survey's sponsor and its two arch-rivals vis-à-vis the ideal

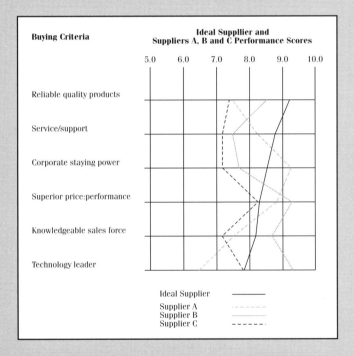

In other words, you could see exactly how the three competitors stacked up, criterion by criterion, so you knew exactly what to stress in your sales and marketing communications. And you had a procedure that you could repeat to measure shifts.

This procedure is of course available to anyone. I've used it successfully with several clients. It's a great way to get a solid grasp of marketplace realities.

Chapter 3

"Who Are Those Guys?"

Executive Summary

Objectives:

(1) Draw out of the universe of potential users, buyers and influencers provided by the situation analysis those "best prospects" to whom it makes sense to communicate.

(2) Get to know these best prospects intimately. Get a feel for them, so you can communicate with them in an easy, familiar way.

Strategies:

(1) Collect and study data that describe the target audience's demographic and psychographic (lifestyle) characteristics.

(2) Review the target audience's attitudes toward your offering vs. rivals.

(3) Identify other attitudes and interests shared by most of the target audience.

(4) Begin to personify the target audience by creating a composite picture of its members.

(5) Conjure up individuals whom you know who are representative of the target audience and so can serve as archetypes.

(6) Empathize with these individuals.

"Damn it, Butch, who are those guys?"

"**W**ho are those guys?" It may be the most important question communications people can ask, even if they're not being chased by the relentless Joe Baltimore and his posse.

Whether you're penning a love letter or an all-points news release, the more you know about the people you're communicating with, the more effective your communication will be. It's that simple.

But what constitutes knowing? And how does one use a situation analysis to help gain this knowledge? These are the questions we'll answer in this chapter...in reverse order.

From situation to target audience

Perhaps the greatest contribution a well-executed situation analysis makes is that, by providing an understanding of all prospects (the universe, if you will), it enables you to prioritize them.

The data will help you define good, better and best prospects for your offering and so identify the people it makes sense to invest time and money talking to about it. These people are the target audience: the folks you want to focus on and learn all you can about.

Knowing = personifying

You know your target audience when you can picture its members in your mind's eye much as you can now picture the people you go to church with, work with or play bridge with. Your target audience, collectively, becomes Cousin Bud and Aunt Ann and the Henreichs from across the street. You're on a first-name basis.

Given that this target audience may number in the millions, it may strike you as a bit of a stretch to try to boil it down to three or four archetypes. But it isn't, really. In fact, it's a straightforward process.

Knowing starts with facts and figures

First, you want to know your target audience's demographic characteristics; that is, how they divide in terms of age, gender, income, occupation, education, family makeup, area of residence, type of residence, et. al.

Second, you want to know their psychographic, or lifestyle, characteristics; that is, how they divide in terms of media consumption habits, entertainment and recreation preferences, civic interests, hobbies, political and religious persuasions, cars, clothes, books, magazines and movies favored, credit cards used and investment activities.

An increasingly important set of lifestyle characteristics revolves around technology ownership and usage: PCs, PDAs, cellular phones, home entertainment systems, digital answering machines. How many in your target audience are online with e-mail addresses? If they're connected, how do they use their connections? For many target audiences today, the Internet is an important shared interest.

Third, you want to know your target audience's attitudes toward your offering vs. its competitors. How aware are they? How familiar? What do they think of it? Feel about it? What do they see as its strengths and weaknesses?

Do these questions sound familiar? They should. We talked about them a chapter ago, regarding the situation analysis, which suggests that you'll find answers to them in your situation analysis.

Ties that bind

Now that you've collected the essential facts and figures, the next step is to identify common threads, qualities that most of the people in your target audience share.

Once you've done this, you'll be able to create a composite, much as a police artist uses descriptions from different witnesses to sketch a suspect. Think about shared interests or attitudes and names and faces of people you're acquainted with come to mind. You've personified your target audience, turned it into people with whom you're on a first-name basis.

You have your archetypes.

For example, my colleagues and I once figured out that a target audience of ours, which numbered in the neighborhood of 5 million people, consisted almost entirely of active individual investors, men and women who took a great interest in their investment portfolios.

It was a short step from this insight to our media director's investment club, a group of men and women who devoted far more attention to their stock portfolios than I do to my checkbook. My art director and I attended a meeting, got to know the members and came away with a personification of our target audience.

Another example: Corporate facilities managers typically decide whose desks, chairs, tables, carpets and filing cabinets their companies will buy. Anxious to find a way to connect with these men and women, a furniture manufacturer hired a psychologist to conduct a series of interviews with them. She reported that the people she talked with shared an important attitude:

Almost to a person, they saw themselves as unsung heroes whose contributions went unnoticed and unappreciated by their superiors, peers and subordinates — corporate Rodney Dangerfields. The furniture maker addressed this shared attitude in its communications and gained market share as a result.

Other common ties that bind: politics, religion, sports, fitness, food (nutrition and cooking), travel, books, movies, cars, gardening, computers, Elvis, Rush Limbaugh, "Car Talk," "A Prairie Home Companion."

When you're looking for ties that bind, here are a couple of things to remember: Shared attitudes (feelings, passions) tend to hold more promise than interests and a good researcher can be very helpful in uncovering them.

Go team, go!

An extraordinary shared passion that you don't need a researcher to uncover: team sports. How do you explain the fact that 50,000 people will brave wind, rain and snow to cheer on their teams? That many will pay outrageous sums to wear their teams' colors? That some will splash their teams' logos on their faces and bodies? Don't even try. But do remember that this shared passion (fanaticism?) might one day give you an opportunity to connect with a target audience.

To reprise

Getting to know your target audience starts with data, facts and figures, about demographics, psychographics and attitudes. As you familiarize yourself with these data, you'll be able to identify shared interests and attitudes, ties that bind. These in turn will enable you to conjure up composites, which will cause familiar names and faces to float to the surface of your mind. When this happens, you know your target audience. Almost.

Context

You have only one more thing to do: determine what they're apt to be doing, thinking, feeling when they receive your communications. Will you catch them en route to or from work, over lunch at work, at home after dinner, in a stuffy hotel meeting room? Will they be alone or in a group? Will your competitors' presentations be nearby?

In the 1968 presidential campaign, Richard Nixon gained an advantage over Hubert Humphrey, according to Joe McGuinness in *The Selling of the President*, when his communications people recognized that most voters mostly saw the candidates from their living rooms (on their TVs). Nixon dialed down, spoke conversationally in his ads as if he were a guest in someone's living room. Humphrey, meanwhile, orated in his TV ads as if he were holding forth in the Hollywood Bowl. And he paid a price. Context is crucial.

Sources

Where do you turn for the basic data you need to start you on the road to composites and personifications? The situation analysis is a key source, particularly if it included a survey of current and prospective users, buyers and influencers.

Additionally, your client may also have useful information — particularly about purchasing habits, purchase frequencies, payment methods. This is especially true if your client offers a frequency program, a la airlines and restaurants. These programs are terrific sources of target audience data. (See chapter 15.)

There are also a great many published sources. Media vehicles can supply you with all sorts of information about their audiences. Government agencies are cornucopias of useful data (e.g., the Census Bureau and the Bureau of Labor Statistics), as are trade associations and universities. And then there's your public library.

There's also your competition, Brand X (and Y and Z), the "other guys" who hawk rival offerings. Check their ads, brochures, videos, data sheets and financial reports. If this makes you uncomfortable, just remember: They're checking everything you put out.

Empathy: the key

Webster defines empathy as "the imaginative projection of a subjective state into an object so that the object appears to be infused with it"; or "the capacity for participation in another's feelings or ideas."

I define it as the ability to walk others' shoes and to see the world through their eyes. And I believe it is a key, if not the key, to creating effective communications. Empathy enables you to get on your target audience's wavelength, to see your offering as they do and to talk with them about it in their terms.

You'll know you know your target audience when you find that you're able to do this, reflexively — when you jump into your target audience's collective head and heart as automatically as your leg jumps when a physician taps your knee with a rubber hammer.

For example, I currently have a composite picture of you in my mind's eye, and whenever I commence writing, this picture comes to mind with no conscious effort on my part. When I sit down to write, I can't keep you from being there. I write to the "you" I see. I write what is, in effect, a letter to the "you" I see, a letter that aims to respond to your interests, concerns and questions.

Chapter 4

"Hot Buttons" and "Seductive Appeals"

Executive Summary

Objective:

Given that you ultimately want your target audience to take some specific action as a consequence of your communications initiative, the task now is to determine what you can say about your offering that will prompt them to do this.

Strategies:

(1) Revisit the situation analysis to see how your target audience views your offering vis-à-vis rivals. Look for points of distinction (they may not exist). But remember that these may not be relevant; i.e., "hot buttons."

(2) Commission research designed to uncover your target audience's hot buttons and get their reactions to possible appeals. Focus group discussions are a good way to do this.

Bear in mind that your target audience may not be able to articulate its real desires, in which case you'll need to make some "brilliant deductions."

(3) Interview the people who designed, engineered and manufacture your offering. They will provide unique and valuable insights, most likely in the form of features ("double ply radial belts").

(4) Collaborate with your research and marketing partners to turn these features into benefits ("80,000 mile guarantee").

(5) Edit your benefit list mercilessly, keeping in mind that your target audience will probably be able to remember three, max.

(6) You've completed this phase when:

- You've built a case that contains one to three benefit-based arguments that tie directly to your target audience's hot buttons;

- each argument is supported by one or two believable, comprehensible features;

- your "summation" issues a clear invitation to your target audience to take the action you want them to.

"Sacre bleu!"

Don't fret. The quest for persuasive arguments is unlikely to require snooping or prove embarrassing. What it requires is digging and more digging.

Yes, you've already collected a ton of data, and you've used it to depict marketplace realities and create personifications of your target audience. Well done. As Joseph Heller says after he's written the first sentence of a novel, you're halfway home.

Now the question is: What is it about your offering that will prompt your target audience to choose it over its rivals? Or, more generally, what is it about your offering that will prompt your target audience to take the action you want them to — *when* you want them to?

Note, these are content questions, "what" questions, not "how" questions. "How" comes later (in chapter nine).

Sources

The answers to these questions lie in three places: the situation analysis, the hearts and minds of the people you want to use/buy your offering, and the hearts and minds of the people who produce it.

The situation analysis will tell how your target audience views your offering vis-à-vis competitors. This enables you to identify points of distinction (if they exist). But it may not tell you how likely these distinctions are to convince your target audience to use/buy your offering. That is, they may not be relevant.

If not, you have a choice. You can make like Sherlock Holmes and do some brilliant deducing. Or you can do research — focus groups with your target audience, for example — and some brilliant deducing.

Remember, you're looking for things you can communicate about your offering that will make it irresistible to your cousin Paul and your Aunt Ann. Remember, too, that cousin Paul and Aunt Ann may not be able to articulate clearly what it is about your offering that makes it irresistible to them.

A few years back, my company was retained to help market 42-day cruises through the South Pacific. When we asked people who had taken this cruise why they did so, they inevitably said things like, "I wanted to see Australia and New Zealand and Tahiti and Fiji" or "I wanted to learn about the exotic cultures of the people of the South Seas."

And yet, when we took the cruise, we noticed that many passengers didn't even leave the ship when it made port. So much for fascinating places and exotic cultures. We decided some in-depth research was in order. It confirmed our suspicions: The ports of call were a rationalization.

What were they really looking for? What were their true "hot buttons?" Number one was the pampering they received aboard ship. Number two was the opportunity to socialize and make new friends. Number three was great food.

So how do you communicate to a target audience that says it wants ports, but really wants service, socializing and eats? In our early efforts, we paid lip service to the ports with a dramatic photograph, then dwelled on the service, society and cuisine in both words and pictures. Later, we got smarter and produced communications that married the four.

Visualize, if you will, a large, luscious photograph that depicts intimate clusters of attractive people socializing on deck at sunset, being served mouth-watering munchies by attentive waiters, with the lush volcanic peak that distinguishes the island of Moorea in the background.

This illustration conveys a key point: the goal is to link your target audience's wants or needs (hot buttons) with your offering's features.

You want to build a case for your offering that plays to their desires.

The third source

No matter that they're biased. No matter that a mile-high wall separates them from users and buyers. The men and women who created your offering can be uniquely helpful when it comes to identifying persuasive arguments for it.

I must acknowledge a bias of my own: I love talking with engineers and product designers. I see them as kindred spirits. And I find that if I'm patient and listen carefully, they'll always give me valuable insights I won't get anywhere else.

I journeyed to the mountains of Idaho one day to interview a reclusive technologist who designed a very sophisticated measuring instrument for scientists and engineers. The trouble was, as elegant it surely was, the people who were supposed to buy it weren't. My mission was to see if I could find some as-yet-undiscovered appeal that would turn the tide.

We sat in the designer's home office and he filled a wall-sized white board explicating his baby to me. I scratched my head. This man wasn't speaking English! But then came the epiphany. We'd been at it for 90 minutes when he revealed it. "You mean none of the competitors have this feature? And it offers these advantages? Wow! Why hasn't anyone told me this before now?"

Previously, I knew what users wanted. Now, I knew how to promise them more of what they wanted and then back up the promise with powerful arguments, bullet-proof validations.

This discovery led to a series of ads in scientific and engineering journals that, according to the publications' readership studies, were better read than the surrounding editorial. It also produced an immediate and sustained jump in product sales.

Moral: Spend time with the people who design, engineer and manufacture your offering. You'll find their views and insights to be unique and invaluable.

Interests, features and benefits

Let's say you're looking for a car that rides smoothly enough to lull your 5-year-old to sleep and firmly enough to allow you to feel in perfect touch with the road. "Smooth but firm," this is what you're interested in — your hot button.

Now what it is about my offering, the Atlantis XL, that addresses your interest? Or, more precisely, what features does the XL possess that will allow me to communicate credibly that it provides a smoother ride and a stronger sense of contact with the road than its competitors?

The situation analysis won't tell me. The target audience can't tell me. The engineers can, but they're likely to respond with engineering features. "The XL's solid-state retro-independent suspension, coupled with its reverse cambered, multi-lobe steering system puts it in a class by itself when it comes to ride and road feel."

Wonderful. But hardly persuasive. These features need to be couched in terms of the benefits they offer users and buyers. And this is something engineers typically aren't very good at.

My theory is, engineers are trained to speak a language — mathematics — that's far more precise than the language of communicators. As a result, they tend to be uncomfortable with our work. We write, "The sun rises in the East." And they want to add precision. "Where in the East? At what time of year? At what time of day? What about cloud cover?"

In an essay in *Forbes/ASAP* magazine, poet-novelist David Berlinski seemed to support this theory when he wrote, "The Polish logician Alfred Tarski demonstrated that the concept of truth could not be defined within any language in which it is expressed."

All of which is to urge you to bear in mind that engineers are great sources and lousy co-editors. They'll tell you about the suspension and steering, but probably not in language your target audience will thrill to.

Turning features into benefits is a job for you and your marketing colleagues.

Another example: Take the mountain bike auxiliary motor I invented two chapters ago. We could talk about its horsepower, weight and dimensions, or we could talk about how handy it is at the end of a long day when you're half a mile from the summit, darkness is falling and your legs feel like fettuccine Alfredo.

Which approach do you guess the target audience will find more compelling?

Arguments (a.k.a. seductive appeals) should consist of benefits that are aligned with the target audience's relevant interests and supported by creditable features. "Attention, marathoners! Do you know why TurboPowerBars give you a quicker, longer-lasting lift? We have the U.S. Food and Drug Administration to thank for the answer. An FDA study found that TurboPowerBars contain twice as many milligrams of complex carbohydrates as their most powerful competitor."

Another personal bias

I believe it pays to know what you're talking about. In fact, as far as I'm concerned, the more you know about your offering, the more effective your communication will be. For me, knowing what you're talking about and cultivating your ability to empathize (chapter three) are the keys to creating effective communications.

I spent too much time in my salad days working with wannabe screenwriters who were biding their time penning copy until they were discovered. They claimed all they needed to know to write great copy were an offering's "selling propositions," the one or two features or ingredients that made it attractive. They would then employ their artistic gifts to dramatize these propositions in ways that made the offering irresistible.

I begged to differ then, and I beg to differ now. The more you know about your offering, I submit, the better your chances of discovering unusual and exciting ways to communicate its relevant benefits…even if you're John Grisham.

Two cases in point: First, for you football fans, John Madden, who's probably the most popular of football's TV commentators. What do you think accounts for his appeal? It's certainly not his mellifluous tones — he sounds like an antique Victrola with a dull needle. Nor is it his scintillating wit — Seinfeld he's not. I think it's because he so obviously knows what he's talking about.

Ideally, you'll know as much about your subject as Coach Madden knows about his.

A writer on the cruise project I mentioned was our equivalent of John Madden. She practically lived with the passengers and crew; she'd hang out in the crew's quarters — like Madden visiting the players' locker rooms. As a result, she gained a fabulous perspective and an enthusiasm that inspired and enlivened her copy.

Now, clearly, you can't talk about your offering's 25,000 horsepower diesel engines if your target audience is interested in service, socializing and good eats. Their wants rule, but a tidbit you pick up in the galley may enable you to talk more persuasively about the delicious cuisine they hunger for.

"Streamlining"

You've hung out with — and listened carefully to — people who speak "foreign" languages: engineers, designers, assemblers, industry analysts, security analysts. You've talked with packagers, shippers, wholesalers, retailers, industry analysts. You've connected with everybody who has a hand in concocting, distributing and evaluating the offering. Now what?

Now it's time to do something that's guaranteed to upset most of your newfound friends. You're going to prioritize the appeals, and then you're going to jettison all but a few of them.

You're going to do this because no matter how gifted you are, your target audience won't remember more than two or three things about your offering. Less is more when it comes to building an irresistible case.

Be ruthless. You can always add back. Try to distill. Or combine. Hone your arguments. Your goal: one to three benefits that tie directly to a target audience desire, supported by a bulletproof feature or two, followed by an invitation to write, call or visit a Web site for details.

These are the makings of an irresistible case.

(They are also the makings of an unhappy client, at least potentially. I know a software developer who simply couldn't abide the reduction of his elegant products down to a trio of sales points. He saw it as caricature and refused to allow it. After a succession of writers had failed to tell the story to his satisfaction, he took pen in hand and did it himself, wrote some of the most reader-unfriendly copy you'll ever see.)

Speeches

If you're creating face-to-face (or virtually face-to-face) presentations, there's something else you can do to make sure you're addressing your audience's interests: You can ask them questions, in advance or on the spot.

I've done both quite successfully. When I'm speaking to an organization or club, I'll draft a brief questionnaire and ask its secretary to deliver it to its members, via fax, e-mail or snail mail. The return address will be mine.

Make the questions interesting and fun, and you'll get grist for your talk and worthwhile insights into the hearts and minds of your audience.

Alternatively, you can pose your questions at the outset of your remarks. I once heard an expert on public speaking say that the first thing a speaker should do to capture an audience's attention is to get them to make a physical movement — raise their hands, wave, tug their left ears or shake hands with a neighbor — and a few introductory questions from you can do this.

"How many of you are driving your dream car?"

I've also been able to involve audiences by addressing open-ended ("What do you think…?") questions to individual members, and by tossing out questions and inviting anyone who wishes to answer.

"If you could do anything you wanted next weekend, what would you do?"

"If you could have dinner with anyone who's alive today, who would it be? What if it were anyone who's ever lived?"

Chapter 5

What Are We Aiming For?

Executive Summary

Objective:

Set realistic, measurable objectives for your communications initiative.

Strategies:

(1) Get clear about the difference between business, marketing and communications objectives.

(2) Understand that all valid communications objectives contain these elements:
- a numerical goal
- a time frame
- a budget

(3) Make sure your communications objectives contain all three elements and that your estimation of the first is realistic.

(4) Understand that communications objectives are route markers, not destinations. They state where you are today and how far you aim to travel within a specific period for a specific investment.

(5) Put together a well-designed benchmark survey mechanism to measure progress. Be certain that it:
- Qualifies respondents as target audience members who have the opportunity to see your communications.
- Asks enough measurement questions to allow you to detect subtle shifts.
- Asks questions that enable you to identify those respondents who genuinely recall your communications.
- Has samples that are large enough to divide into subsamples whose responses are likely to be statistically significant.

(6) Present your initiative to your managers in a way that allows them to compare its financial contribution to the organization with those of other initiatives from other departments.

(7) Make it clear to them that you can predict how many leads, calls, Web site hits and/or predisposition points your initiative will deliver per dollar per year, and that you can estimate the financial value of these results to the organization.

(8) If you doubt your ability to do this, ask only for funding for a test, then implement your initiative in one market (geographic or demographic) under tight controls and use the results either to buttress your position or rethink it.

"Yes, Fuddly, it's great all right. But what's the ROI?"

The eternal question. Everyone who has ever considered investing in a communications effort has asked it. Few have been satisfied with the response.

You've no doubt heard retail czar John Wannamaker's famous observation: "I know half of what I spend on advertising is wasted. I just don't know which half." He said this more than 70 years ago, but he or his successors could easily have said it yesterday. Some things never change.

Until now. By the time you've read this chapter, you'll be able to answer the eternal question…almost. That is, you'll come a lot closer than most.

Needed: careful definitions

Who knows why, but the word "objective" seems to cause the clearest of communicators to go cloudy, like somebody slipped a mickey into their latte. Two sorts of confusions are typical:

First, they tend to confuse business or marketing objectives with communications objectives.

(Do you? Let's see. Is this a business objective, a marketing objective or a communications objective? "Increase share from 10.5 percent to 11.5 percent within 12 months." If you answered, "marketing," go to the head of the class.)

A communications objective, by definition, focuses exclusively on what a communications initiative, by itself, seeks to achieve. "Sell 50 widgets this weekend" isn't a communications objective unless yours is a direct response initiative, and your communications are surrogates for salespeople.

How about this? "Prompt 50 people who have taken at least one previous cruise to call a toll-free number this weekend for information about our June 15 South Pacific cruise." This is almost a communications objective. (See below.)

Confusion two

Communications people too often write communications objectives that aren't measurable. "Build positive awareness and generate qualified leads." Yuck! That's not an objective. That's mush. What constitutes being "positively aware?" How much do you aim to build? How long do you plan to take? How much do you plan to spend? What's a "qualified lead?" How many do you intend to generate? By when?

VIP (very important point): Good communications objectives aren't destinations. They're route markers. They state where you are today and how far you aim to travel within a specific period given a specific investment.

For example: "We'll invest $100,000 in an ad blitz that will prompt 50 people who have taken at least one cruise to call a toll-free number this weekend for information about our June 15 South Pacific cruise."

This is a bona fide communications objective. It contains the three elements that all valid communications objectives must:

- a goal (50 people);
- a time frame (this weekend);
- a budget.

If your communications objectives don't have these three elements, shred them.

Another example

"Currently, 15 percent of all CIOs at Fortune 500 companies know that our B-100 offers a 33 percent price:performance advantage over our nearest competitor. Given a marketing communications investment of $4 million per year, 50 percent of them will know this one year from now. Two years out, the figure will be 70 percent."

Communications objectives like this will bring joy to your bean counters' hearts, if not smiles to their faces. Now you can tell them that an investment of X dollars will move the needle Y distance over Z time frame...and that you'll monitor your program's performance and provide tracking reports semi-annually.

No, this is not a dollars-and-cents ROI, but it's close. It provides general managers the sort of information they need to make an informed decision. That is, they can now decide how important it is that 70 percent of all Fortune 500 CIOs know that the company's B-100 offers a 33 percent price:performance edge, and then approve or disapprove the investment.

Data like these also give managers a more informed way to evaluate investments in communications initiatives relative to investments in other activities or programs. This strengthens the communicator's hand. Why? Because it reduces the disadvantage most communications people face when they present their plans to their general managers.

As you know, these managers typically receive proposals from all who report to them, and most include ROI forecasts.

"Adding a third converter masher to the No. 2 line in plant No. 7 will double production within six months at a cost of $1.64 million. Given current margins, this translates into $4.59 million net after the first year. Give or take half a percent, of course."

Now, how does a communications person compete with this department head for available dollars? By spelling out the goal, the time frame and the required investment…in quantifiable terms. And by demonstrating how he or she intends to measure progress at regular intervals.

So how do you measure progress at regular intervals? By fielding a benchmark survey of your target audience before your program breaks and then repeating it as your program unfolds.

About benchmarks

They are crucial. Perhaps that's why they're usually designed poorly, conducted thoughtlessly and repeated too frequently. It's sad and ironic that because they're ill-conceived, benchmark surveys often sink the programs they're designed to save.

So what does a well-conceived benchmark look like? First, it poses at least six questions to measure progress — and more is better, because shifts are apt to be slight.

Second, it includes at least three questions designed to establish genuine awareness of the communications initiative.

Third, it includes qualifying questions to ensure that all respondents are in fact target audience members who will be or have been exposed to the communications.

Finally, it queries enough of these target audience members to enable them to be divided into two statistically significant groups for analysis: those who recall the communications and those who don't.

It is the differences between these two groups that are the key measurements, not the those between the pre- and post-launch samples. Pre/post comparisons let you take into consideration what happened in your marketplace, generally in the interval between surveys.

Let's get specific

You're the marketing director for Mount Aux, the company that markets auxiliary motors for mountain bikes. You want to run a three-year, $3 million ad campaign in the leading mountain bike retailer trade magazine.

Your objective is to convince 30 percent of the 12,500 men and women who run North American mountain bike retail stores to designate your company, Mount Aux, as a "preferred supplier" within one year, 50 percent within two years, 65 percent within three years.

You know that 5 percent have currently awarded Mount Aux this designation, and that the Mountain Bike Retailers Association has stipulated that suppliers must meet five criteria to earn it.

- 24-hour product support policy
- 15-day payment policy
- no-questions-asked return policy
- quarterly incentive programs
- co-op ad programs

Now what should your benchmark survey questionnaire look like? It should lead off with questions that establish that the respondent runs a mountain bike retail store and is a regular reader of your ad vehicle.

Second, it should ask as many as a dozen questions that pertain to the preferred supplier criteria; e.g., how do you rate, on a 1–5 scale with 1 being unacceptable and 5 being exceptional, the following three suppliers in terms of their product support policy? Their payment policy? Etc.

Third, it should conclude with three or four questions regarding ad recall; e.g., have you noticed any advertising run by any of these three suppliers lately? If yes, where? Can you describe it? Anything else? Do you recall the theme? How would you rate it on our 1–5 scale? Etc.

Fourth, if the sample size for your first survey is, say, 400, the sample size for subsequent iterations (waves) should be at least 650.

What does this give you?

Consider what the results of the first two waves of the benchmark I've described might look like.

	Wave 1	Wave 2 Non-Recallers	Wave 2 Recallers	Shift
Sample size	400	400	250	
Know enough to rate	40%	44%	64%	+20%
Ratings				
Support policy	3.6	3.9	4.3	+14%
Payment policy	3.2	3.3	4.3	+30%
Return policy	3.4	3.4	4.0	+18%
Incentive policy	3.1	3.3	3.9	+18%
Co-op policy	3.3	3.5	4.2	+20%

Let's say you fielded Wave 2 six months after you launched your ad program. You'd have solid evidence that it was performing well.

Please note, I snuck a line in on you, "Know enough to rate." This is a key measure for a new company such as Mount Aux because it's an indicator of familiarity. And as research guru Daniel Yankelovich has observed, "Familiarity breeds favorability."

Please remember, also, that not everyone who reads a publication you're advertising in (or listens to a radio station you're advertising on) belongs to your target audience. So you can't assume that you've qualified your sample adequately when you establish that they're regular readers (or listeners).

I made this mistake for years and lost good programs as a consequence. Be careful. For a benchmark design we just completed, the magazines that will carry the advertising are to provide the research firm subscriber lists broken out by SIC codes and job titles. Given that we used SIC codes and job titles to define our target audience, this will allow us to prequalify survey respondents.

To anticipate a question I suspect you have at this point: Unless your initiative is an all-out blitz, don't field Wave 2 until it's been running for at least six months; even then, your (and your managers') expectations should be modest. Best case, you'll wait a year.

Predicting

How does one set realistic communications objectives? How does one know that 50 veteran cruise vacationers should call in response to a $100,000 ad blitz? Why not 100? 500? Here are six ways to get answers:

- Use history as your guide. How many responses have other, similar investments pulled?
- Ask the media for help. Their representatives maintain case histories to help them demonstrate the power of their particular vehicles, and they're happy to share them.
- Turn to your colleagues in noncompetitive companies — perhaps through associations you belong to. (This is a good reason to join and participate in associations, by the way.)
- Turn to associations your firm belongs to (e.g., The Cruise Lines International Association).
- Contact college professors who teach business, marketing or advertising courses. Your need may become a student project.
- Test your initiative. Implement it in Peoria or in a particular edition of a magazine for three to six months and see what happens.

Is the eternal question unanswerable?

Can one calculate financial returns on investments in communications? Yes. Direct marketers do it all the time. For example, the people who sell exercise machines and beauty creams via infomercials on late-night television know exactly what the return is on their communications investment.

But for those of us who aren't in the direct marketing business, it's another story. When the objective is something other than cash on the barrelhead, I believe it's impossible to quantify a financial ROI because the dollar value of successful communications initiatives varies from case to case.

Example: The defense electronics division of an international technology company aims to generate 50 percent of its revenues from companies in the private sector seven years out, up from zero today.

To achieve this, the division must predispose many time-constrained, information-overladen people who are unfamiliar with it and familiar with its competitors to consider doing business with it.

Obviously, in this instance, a percentage point's worth of familiarity is worth a lot of money, and communications can deliver it. How much money? That's for division management to decide.

Contrast this with another division in the same company. It's already a market leader. Its products hold dominant market shares. For it, a percentage point increase in predisposition is worth much less. Even so, its general manager insists on investing in communications designed to do just that. Why? He wants to protect and reinforce the position his division has worked so hard to achieve.

Study your business situation. Determine how a communications program that fulfilled management's every desire would affect it. Then talk with management about those effects. You'll quickly capture their attention and interest.

Chapter 6

Time and Money

Executive Summary

Objective:

Determine how much money and time it's appropriate to invest in your communications initiative.

Strategies:

(1) Triangulate. That is, approach this determination in three ways:

- Focus on the problem or opportunity your initiative addresses, estimate the dollars involved and relate your budgets to them.

  Example: If the stakes are $10 million over one year, it makes sense to invest $1 million to $2 million to collect them.

- Focus on the likely consequences if your initiative succeeds and relate your budgets to them.

  Example: Let's say your initiative promises to generate 1,000 qualified leads per week and your salespeople typically turn one in five leads into customers who spend $500 per year, on average, 25 percent of which falls to the bottom line.

  This means your initiative will produce an estimated $2.3 million in incremental earnings…and warrants an investment of half this amount (assuming there are other costs involved in booking this new business).

- Focus on what it will take in terms of time and money to make your initiative successful.

  Example: Multiply the number of people in your target audience by the cost to produce and distribute to them the messages that will move them to think, feel or act as you want.

(2) You now have three time/money estimates. If they're close, your job is done. If there's a big spread, go with your first number and adjust the dimensions of your initiative to fit.

"And the secret word is…"

The cantankerous Groucho Marx promised his "You Bet Your Life" guests $100 if they said the secret word. In this chapter, we'll go Groucho one better and offer two secret words. The first is…

Appropriate

As in, what are the appropriate time and money budgets for your communications initiative…given the problem it aims to help solve or the opportunity it aims to help exploit?

Please note, we're not talking about communications objectives; we're talking about business circumstances — problems, opportunities and capabilities. When it comes to setting time/money budgets, they are your point of departure.

A war story

No matter that a decade has passed and taken much water under the bridge with it. I can still taste the moment of my downfall. We were competing for an investor relations assignment from a pre-eminent distribution company. After several meetings, I was invited to what I anticipated would be a victory lunch in the firm's executive dining room.

After a pleasantry or two, the company's CFO asked me how much he ought to set aside for the first year's investor relations effort. I estimated the size of the target audience and the cost of producing and distributing the requisite communications and gave him a "horseback" estimate.

He looked at me as if I'd lost my mind. "That's half our profits," he snapped.

Gulp. I'd focused so completely on what mattered to me — target audience, message creation/production/distribution — that I neglected to even consider what mattered to him: earnings. And it cost my company a nifty assignment.

Triangulation

The second secret word, triangulation, is both a pitfall avoidance procedure and the best way to make sure your time/money budgets are appropriate. As you might expect, it's a three-step process:

Step One: Focus on the problem or opportunity your initiative addresses, estimate the dollars involved and relate your budgets to them.

Step Two: Focus on the likely financial consequences if your initiative succeeds as planned and relate your budgets to them.

Step Three: Focus on what it will take in terms of money and time to move your target audience to think, feel or act as you want — given your situation analysis and your definitions of the target audience, the arguments and the objectives.

You now have three estimates. If they're close, your job is done. If there's a big spread, go with your first number and adjust the dimensions of your initiative to fit.

For example

Suppose a city council in one of your plant communities is threatening to close down your operation because, the council says, it's leaking toxic chemicals that could poison the town's drinking water.

Your company's executives all agree that the threat is serious and that the company stands to lose $1 million per week in profits if it's carried out. They also fear it could set a precedent that could threaten the company's other four plants.

You point out that the company paid for an independent study that found no evidence of leaks and that the state environmental protection agency gave the plant a clean bill of health a year ago. You recommend a communications blitz to make sure every member of the community understands these two points.

Your CFO asks you, "How much do you figure it'll cost?" You triangulate.

First, you calculate the potential cost of the problem. Huge — $1 million a week in profits. Not to mention the adverse impact on the other plants. Conclusion: It makes sense to invest a lot of money in a blitz. As much as $3 million would certainly be appropriate (assuming, of course, that the company had no cheaper options, such as legal action).

Second, you calculate the financial impact of success — $1 million profit dollars a week preserved — and you're assured again that $2 million to $3 million is appropriate.

Third, you calculate what it will take to be successful. You multiply the target audience (community members) by the number of messages you want to deliver by the cost of delivering them.

Say the community's adult population is 500,000, and you want to send each of them five personal letters, first class, on your company's letterhead, one a day for five consecutive days. Figure 32 cents postage and 18 cents to cover stationery, stuffing, handling and copywriting. Five letters multiplied by 500,000 at 50 cents postage and handling per letter equals $1,250,000.

Let's say, too, that you want the company to host televised public forums on five consecutive nights — "town hall meetings" that feature the two scientists who conducted your study, the plant manager, three plant workers and your CEO. You figure it will cost $500,000 to transport, accommodate and compensate the scientists, rent a hall, buy TV time and run announcement/invitation ads.

Finally, you want the scientists and your CEO to participate in private meetings with the local newspaper's editorial board, the news directors of the local TV and radio stations, the head of the local chapter of the Sierra Club and civic leaders from local churches, businesses and schools. Estimated cost: $250,000.

Total cost of the blitz so far: $2 million. But that's not what you tell the CFO. Yes, it's an appropriate figure. But it lacks one thing. A contingency.

Always add a contingency. Always. How large? Ideally, 20 percent, but in no case less than 10 percent. This takes the estimated cost of your blitz to $2,200,000. And that's the number you give your CFO…after you remind him of the stakes, of course, $1 million a week in earnings, plus an incalculable ripple effect.

Estimating the cost of success

The second thing you focus on when you triangulate is the financial contribution your communications initiative is likely to make if it's successful. When you do this, don't forget to consider questions such as:

- If your initiative generates 100 qualified leads per week, will your salespeople be able to handle them? If not, how many new leads per week could they handle?
- If you get the conversions you anticipate, will your manufacturing and distribution operations be able to fill the orders in a timely fashion? If not, how many incremental orders per week could they fill?
- How about your tech reps? How many new accounts can they support without staffing up?
- How long will it take to gear up to handle the new accounts your initiative will produce?

Answers to these questions will help you avoid a cardinal sin: getting too far out in front of your operating people.

The other end of the 'scope'

Another word of caution: When you estimate what's required to implement your initiative successfully given target audience size, arguments and objectives, be sure to revisit your situation analysis.

Pay particular attention to competitors' perceived strengths, their marketing and communications activities (the "noise level") and all other marketplace realities you can think of. Time of year, which could lead to tie-ins with other promotions and events (e.g., Fourth of July and Presidents' Day sales; Mother's Day, Father's Day and Back to School promotions).

Then ask yourself — given all these realities — what will it really take, in money and time, to move your target audience to think, feel or act as you want?

To a degree, this is a guess on your part. But if you've done your homework, it will be a highly educated guess, a "professional judgment." If you've followed the blueprint, by the time you get to the time/money budget phase, you've developed a solid feel for the circumstances and what's needed to deal with them. In your gut, you know. Don't be afraid to trust it.

Downscaling

What if you conclude that it's not appropriate to invest the time and money you need for your initiative to succeed? How do you regroup? Where do you start?

With your target audience. Shrink it. Instead of targeting all 500,000 plant community adults, aim at the 200,000 who have college degrees, or the 125,000 who have school-aged kids. Or the 75,000 who subscribe to the local newspaper.

Compromise coverage (reach), never frequency. If your budget is 30 percent too high, simply reduce coverage of your target audience by about that percentage. Do not reduce the number of times you talk with them. Given the "noise level" — the large number of messages others also are beaming at your audience, repetition is essential. Otherwise, you just won't get heard.

Incidentally, one way to reduce reach is cut back geographically; e.g., by concentrating on large metro areas. Another way is to trim your initiative demographically; e.g., by focusing exclusively on those members of your target audience who own homes, are under 50, drive imported cars...whatever.

Just make sure that when you scale back the dimensions of your initiative, you also scale back its objectives. And verify that all interested parties understand and agree to your downscaled objectives...lest you get burned after the fact.

Another war story

Everything you've read in this chapter pertains to determining two budgets: a dollar budget and a time budget. The latter is just as important as the former. When you estimate your time budget, two considerations are often at odds:

- How much time you think it will take to achieve your objectives.
- How long the marketplace will give you to achieve your objectives.

When these two conflict, the second must take precedence or the consequences can be dire.

A client friend tells of the time he called his ad agency to ask for a special merchandising program that he could unveil at his annual mid-June dealer breakfast in Chicago. The agency went to work and cooked up a doozy of a program. My friend was thrilled. "How soon can you have it ready?" he asked. "July 1," answered his account exec.

This benighted account exec forgot the most important thing: his client's needs. Don't make this mistake. Remember, all problems are time bombs, and all opportunities are windows.

The creative variable

We won't get to communications strategies for a couple of chapters. Nonetheless, when you're setting time/money budgets, you should bear in mind that the quality of your messages — their ability to attract and hold the target audience's attention, their credibility, memorability and persuasiveness — will determine how much bang your budgets will buy.

Hence, it's important to factor them into your time/money budget deliberations. But how? Ultimately, you'll have to make a judgment call, but there may be data that can help you. Check out recent history. You may have studies that report on message reaction and recall.

If your initiative includes advertising, for example, you may have ad recall studies that show the scores your company's ads have posted. (This is a big deal. Remember, ads recalled by 50 percent of your target audience are worth twice as much as ads recalled by 25 percent.)

You may have a sense, based on the arguments you've defined, that you're sitting on some especially dramatic news that will be instantly memorable and persuasive as soon as your target audience sees or hears it. Be careful here. But if you're convinced, you can reduce your time/money budgets.

Finally, it may be that you have great confidence in the artistry of the men and women who will turn your arguments into ads, videos, speeches, presentations or brochures. You just know they'll come up with something stupendous. Maybe you've done some preliminary brainstorming with them and you're all excited. Again, I urge you to discount your excitement by 50 percent, but you should by all means take it into account when you're setting your initiative's time/money budgets.

The Jordan factor

When you're thinking about the appropriate investment in your communications initiative, don't be shy. The contribution it makes to your organization, its return, may indeed justify (or even demand) a huge outlay. If so, propose it, unreservedly.

If you need moral support, imagine that you're Michael Jordan's agent. When you sit with the general manager of the Chicago Bulls, you ask for $25 million without batting an eye. When you meet with the people at Nike, it's $40 million. You tell the Gatorade people that your client's services will cost them $20 million, and your heart rate doesn't budge.

Why not? Because in the same breath, you remind these clients that Michael Jordan earns them 50 times what he costs them.

Don't forget that your communications initiative could do the same sort of thing for your organization. And don't forget to mention it.

Chapter 7

The Personality Behind the Voice

Executive Summary

Objective:

Gain a clear understanding of the personality of the sponsor of your initiative so that your communications will be appropriate and ring true.

Strategies:

(1) Begin by bearing three things in mind:

- If people in an organization feel uncomfortable about a communications initiative, it's in trouble, no matter how effectively it's performing in the marketplace.

- An organization's personality is difficult to define because an organization is inherently complex, dynamic and amorphous. You have to dig deep to find "eternal verities."

- While everyone involved in an organization has a view of its personality, most of these people also have axes to grind, which will color their vision.

(2) The best way to grasp an organization's personality is to travel wide and burrow deep.

- Read as much as you can, including puff stuff. (Especially puff stuff!)

- Talk to as many people as you can at all levels: employees, dealers, directors, suppliers, retirees — one-on-one and in groups.

- Hang out on shop floors, in cafeterias, in wholesale and retail outlets, with logistics and transportation people. Eavesdrop. Watch how they treat one another.

- Pay attention to architecture, interior design, graphics, furniture, furnishings and parking lots (who drives what?).

- Engage top management in depth, particularly the CEO. CEOs' perspectives are, by definition, unique because their responsibilities are unique.

- Make it clear that you regard the CEO as your co-author and that you have to get beyond boilerplate and "official" party lines to do a first-class job for the organization.

- Talk to secretaries. They're almost always smart, perceptive and plugged in. They will tell you what the organization is really all about, what its personality really is.

- Once you think you've got a fix on your organization's personality, sketch out a few thumbnail prototypes that express it and show them to your CEO. Keep it informal. You're not looking for approvals, just gut reactions.

- Repeat this process until you have a "tone of voice" that's consistent with the organization's personality.

*"Let me assure you, as sure as my name is Ralph Waldo Emerson,
organizations have personalities just like individuals do.
And they're usually split."*

You know the situation: who you're talking to, what you're talking about, what you're trying to achieve and how much time and money you have to achieve it. Now it's time to consider one of those "little big things" that can really trip you up.

Who are you talking for?

Communications Boot Hill is full of seemingly brilliant communications initiatives that bit the dust because employees or dealers or board members said, "It's just not us."

No matter that they were performing effectively in the marketplace.

How do you figure out just who is "us"? It's not easy. If the organization you're working with is typical, just about everyone in it has her or his own idea about its personality. All are worth listening to. When it comes to divining an organization's personality, more is more. So listen widely, and be careful not to tie yourself too closely to any particular point of view. Otherwise, something like this might happen to you.

A face full of egg

The product, a high-performance device for engineers, suffered from a 20 percent price:performance *disadvantage*. Our assignment was to overcome this disadvantage by developing an argument (seductive appeal) that would persuade the hyper-analytical target audience to pay the premium.

We repositioned the product as an "engineering work of art." We talked about the "hierarchy of concepts that underlies the functions," the "precision" and the "harmony of art."

"Bravo!" cried the marketing, sales and communications people. "Well done!" echoed the product management people. They ran ads, put out brochures, flyers and videos. And the target audience responded. Many leads. Lots of buzz.

Then came word from the executive suite: "Kill it." It seems the men at the top, whom we had ignored when we created the initiative, concluded that it ran counter to what company was all about: analytical devices for analytical engineers. "We make tools," they reasoned, "not works of art."

And that was that. Another candidate for Communications Boot Hill.

The point is, the mistake was ours. We followed the path of least resistance, assumed that the people we were dealing directly with — marketing, sales, product management — understood the company's personality, when in fact they were focused on a price:performance problem that threatened their livelihoods.

They would have gone for go-go dancers popping out of giant cupcakes if they thought it would fix the problem.

Moral: Listen to everybody you can, particularly everybody who has an interest in your initiative. Be sure to include others who communicate on the company's behalf — speech writers, ad writers, the people who publish the organization's newsletters. Be alert for differing views. And bear in mind that just about everybody you talk with has an ax to grind.

Other things you can do

Between listenings, read everything you can get your hands on by and about the organization you're talking for. Even puff stuff. Indeed, especially puff stuff. It will give you a sense of how the organization wants to be viewed. Company histories, founders' autobiographies (hagiographies, really), executives' speeches — all are useful.

Between listenings and readings, hang out on shop floors, in cafeterias, in wholesale and retail outlets, with logistics and transportation people. Eavesdrop. Notice how these people treat one another.

Take special note of the organization's architecture, interior design, corporate graphics, furniture, furnishings, the kinds of cars in the parking lots.

Do the suits drive Buicks or BMWs? How about the product design and engineering people?

You've read, listened and hung out. You've gotten a bunch of differing, and competing, views. And you've concluded that Freud himself couldn't psyche out an entity as complex, dynamic and amorphous as your organization.

Don't despair

Persist. Get yourself invited to a function that your outfit puts on for retirees. Most have no axes to grind, few inhibitions and terrific perspectives.

That's true for an organization's long-time ("seasoned") veterans as well, be they employees, dealers, directors or suppliers (especially those from the organization's legal counsel and ad agencies).

I've often found that my clients' work forces include what I call "keepers of the flame," people who, officially or unofficially, take it upon themselves to maintain organizational histories. They're always worth a visit.

In one case, the keeper of the flame was the company's patent attorney. It was a perfect match of profession and avocation. The right man in the right place. He saw — correctly — that the company's patent history identified and opened the door to nearly every noteworthy development.

As you read, talk, listen, hang out and nose around, remember that the people you're watching and engaging constitute an "over the shoulder" target audience for you. They will see your communications, and if too many of them get uncomfortable, you're in trouble. They have life-and-death power over your work.

The case of Father Sarducci

It was an inspired solution. Father Guido Sarducci, a fictional Roman Catholic priest created by comedian/actor Don Novello, would talk inexpertly and hilariously about our client's less than scintillating product features and benefits. He'd bring them to life. Sales, marketing, communications and product management loved the idea. So did the CEO. But it almost wasn't enough.

When the company's employees learned that a pseudo priest was going to be a company spokesman, some of them argued so vociferously that this ran counter to the company's personality that the bosses almost changed their minds. All that saved the program was an 11th-hour survey by us that demonstrated that the good Father offended none of the company's constituencies…and amused all of them (except for the complaining employees, of course).

Included in this demonstration were interviews my wife and I conducted in two Catholic church parking lots on a Sunday morning. We even talked with parish priests who thought Father Sarducci was a fine and funny fellow.

Two things you must do

There are a half-dozen or so people in any organization who are often ignored and almost inevitably have unique perspectives. An unhappy tale will introduce one of them.

Rob, the company's new corporate communications vice president, was intelligent, capable and professed to have the CEO's ear. When he outlined the company's plan to reposition itself, I was impressed.

"The boss wants a full-blown program to communicate this new direction to all the company's constituents," Rob said. "We're going all out."

What an opportunity! We turned ourselves inside out and came up with a soup-to-nuts campaign that Rob labeled "stupendous." The next step was to show it to the CEO. "He'll love it," said Rob.

Big meeting. CEO, COO, strategic planning VP, a couple of group heads. Rob sets the stage. We unveil our artistry — ads, TV spots, new company magazine, posters, contests, buttons, banners, the works. When we finish, silence.

Finally, the CEO speaks. "What's this all about, Rob?"

Long pause.

"It's our new direction."

"But, Rob, I don't want to go in a new direction."

End of stupendous campaign. Yet another candidate for Communications Boot Hill.

Moral: Until you've talked to the boss, you're not ready to put pen to paper.

Feet up, hair down

I worked for a decade with a very wise CEO who spent hours at the outset of our relationship reminiscing about the history of the company and the personalities of its key people through the ages. He also talked candidly about his own personality and his idiosyncrasies and eccentricities.

I'll always remember the day I met him for the first time. It was a Tuesday afternoon. I was his last appointment and he went on at such length — four hours — that I missed my flight home and he was late for his dinner engagement.

He talked about the founders, his predecessors, his triumphs, failures and frustrations, his hopes, dreams and plans, his mom, dad, brothers and kids.

He told stories, marvelous tales, always tied somehow to the company and its people. I just listened, and nodded my head from time to time. It was clear that there was a method in his meandering: to prepare me to write on the company's behalf. He reckoned his job was to maintain and enhance the health of his enterprise, and he believed communications could help.

As it turned out, it was a good investment of time for him, and a great one for me. I learned exactly who I was talking for. I knew the company's heart and soul.

They want to be involved

You might be saying to yourself, "Our CEO is too busy to talk with my group about communications initiatives. He/she sees that as our job." And you might be right. But if you are, your CEO is a rare bird. Most love to involve themselves in creating their organization's communications initiatives for at least six reasons:

- All communications, by definition, reflect the organization's character and stature and so will affect its reputation — something every CEO cares a great deal about.

- Most communications are public, visible not only to their target audiences but to anyone else who happens on them or seeks them out. Hence, they can cause damage if they're not carefully vetted. And who better to do that than the CEO?

- CEOs are paid to develop, hone and articulate their organization's vision and reason for being, and communications initiatives give them a chance to do this.

- As communications are a very visible expense, hence easy targets for critics, it behooves CEOs to get involved so they can better defend the outlay if they have to.

  (One CEO co-author used to calculate darn near everything in terms of "earnings per share" because that's how his performance was measured. We'd show him a budget and he'd say, "Hmm, two cents a share.")

- Communications sessions are a lot more fun than just about everything else a CEO has to do (e.g., budget negotiations). Getting involved offers a refreshing change of pace.

- Creating communications is an activity that most CEOs think they're good at even if they profess not to be. (And, in my experience, they usually are. They've certainly helped me.)

The essential others

They're unglamorous, invisible, seemingly innocuous and absolutely plugged into what's really going on, what the organization is really all about. They're secretaries (or "administrative assistants" in today's parlance).

You'll learn more about an organization's personality from three or four of its secretaries than you will from any single person save the CEO. They're smart, perceptive and they don't miss a thing. Don't miss listening to them.

Fast tracking

Are you thinking that it would take years to do all the things I've suggested in this chapter? You're probably right. And that's not a problem if you intend to work with the sponsoring organization on an ongoing basis. You do what you can as you can, and learn from your misfires.

But there is something that'll accelerate the process: Marry your quest for the organization's personality to your pursuit of the other definitions called for by the blueprint. When you're reading, listening, hanging out and nosing around to collect marketplace realities, target audience attitudes and arguments, look for personality info at the same time.

Given the linearity of print, I'm forced to lay out sequentially a series of steps that can easily overlap. Obviously, given the nature of all communications initiatives, the more you can do at one time, the better.

Trials and errors

The best way to find an appropriate communications style isn't pretty. It's through trial and error, preferably working directly with your CEO co-author, candidly and informally, just as ghostwriters work with their clients. (A ghostwriter is in fact what you are, at least at this point in the communications-building process).

Don't be reluctant to try out your ideas and opinions. When you think you have a fix on the organization's personality, sketch out a few thumbnail prototypes that express it, and show them to your CEO co-author. Keep it informal. You're not looking for approvals, just gut reactions.

Repeat as necessary until you have a "tone of voice" that's consistent with the organization's personality.

She who pays the piper calls the tune

When it comes to finding an appropriate "voice," you'll almost certainly run into heartfelt differences of opinion. Testing alternatives can ease these differences, as can patient, no-holds-barred discussions that allow dissenters to vent.

But you can't depend on these tactics to get you where you have to be. And you can't compromise ("we'll be tough and resolute this month, sensitive and compassionate next month"). Someone has to pull rank. And this someone should be the person who's funding your initiative.

Listen to everyone. Try hard to reconcile the differences. But at the end of the day, heed whoever's paying the bill.

Chapter 8

Matters of Fact and Opinion

Executive Summary

Objective:

Be as sure as you can that the cornerstones of your communications initiative are rock solid.

Strategies:

(1) Identify "fact gaps" in your situation analysis and cornerstone definitions, and commission research studies to fill them.

(2) Make sure the studies' methodologies, sample sizes and compositions, questionnaires and analytical techniques are such that you can have confidence in — and defend — their findings. Don't cut corners. Half-baked research is worse than no research.

(3) Test questionnaires and revise and retest them until you're sure they're free of ambiguity. Remember, your findings are only as reliable as your questionnaire is clear.

(4) Resist efforts by colleagues and superiors to take short cuts, either by forgoing research or compromising its quality. Remind them that the cost of ignorance is high.

An out-of-focus ad, brochure, video, TV spot or sales presentation means many wasted media and production dollars, not to mention underwhelmed target audiences.

Quote the refrain from the classic calypso ballad, "House built on a weak foundation will not stand." Or quote the famous striptease artist Gypsy Rose Lee, who said, "Anything worth doing well is worth doing slowly."

If your colleagues and superiors remain unconvinced, read the rest of this chapter.

"Don't confuse me with the facts. I know what I want."

L et's review the bidding.

You've completed a **situation analysis** that lays the groundwork for your communications initiative.

You've drawn cornerstone definitions that set a solid foundation for it:

- **Target audience**
- **Arguments** ("seductive appeals" to "hot buttons")
- **Objective/Budget/Time frame**
- **Personality**

Now it's time to step back and ask two questions:

- How solid are the cornerstones, really?
- How enthusiastically are they endorsed by the people you're working with and for (a.k.a. the "interested parties")?

These are critical issues, given that you plan to build a comprehensive (and expensive) communications initiative on your cornerstones, and that you'll need the support of the interested parties to implement it successfully.

Happily, you can do one thing that will address both issues. Commission research, designed and conducted by independent professionals, to fill gaps with facts.

I think I can. I know I can.

Get the facts. Accept no substitutes. Don't content yourself with "informed opinions," "educated guesses" and "professional judgments." Knowing beats thinking 10 times out of 10.

In theory, no one would disagree with this, right? But in practice, getting from thinking to knowing — when it involves commissioning research — is often easier said than done. You've heard the arguments for "compromise" and "going with our gut."

Is there a marketer in the house?

A father-and-son team of dentists comes up with a nifty idea: put together a national network of dentists by forming a corporation that acquires independent dental offices around the country.

Member dentists retain their autonomy while benefiting from huge economies of scale. Lab work, accounting, purchasing, marketing, pensions, benefits, even magazine subscriptions are all handled centrally by a corporate staff. The improved margins fund research, training, advanced education, exchanges of ideas and techniques, development of new technologies and, of course, immodest shareholder dividends.

Patients who avail themselves of member dentists' services benefit from consistently superior care wherever they happen to be. If you get a splitting toothache on the road, the local member dentist you see finds out all about you simply by calling up your oral history on the office computer (purchased, of course, at a large discount by the folks at corporate).

You now have the picture. Now for the $64 question: Should the corporation have a brand identity or should it be invisible to consumers? The Starbucks of dental services? Or a behind-the-scenes operator a la Procter & Gamble? There's only one way to get a reliable answer: Ask your current and potential patients. Commission an in-depth market research study. There's a lot riding on the answer, and teasing reliable reactions out of people will be tricky.

But this is a marketer speaking, and dentists don't think like marketers. They recognized the importance of the question, of course, but their way of coming up with the answer was to talk with one another. The company's founders called together its employee shareholders, asked them what they thought and went with the consensus view.

Which was? I'm tempted not to tell you because it's irrelevant. The point isn't the answer, but how they got it. But I'll resist the temptation. In their wisdom, they opted to be invisible.

Some of your colleagues and superiors may argue, "We live in an imperfect world. You can't know everything. And besides, we're committed to launch our 'new and improved' XL-200 in 90 days."

Others may argue that the research will take too much time and cost too much money: "We already know enough to make realistic assumptions."

Still others may reason, "We already know what we need to, thanks to the survey we did five years ago."*

And a final band of naysayers may simply contend, "You can't believe what research tells you anyhow."

In this chapter, I'll argue that commissioning research to fill in "fact gaps" is critical. I'll give you arguments you can use when you encounter resistance. And I'll review a variety of research methods, so you'll have some guidelines once you've overcome it.

Why it matters

Let's start with a true story. Only the names have been changed to protect the mortified:

Marketing director Barry invites marketing consultant Don to a get-acquainted meeting. Aiming to create a congenial mood, Don drops the second syllable from Barry's name, calls him "Bear" throughout their get-together. Afterwards, Barry tells an aide that no one has ever called him "Bear" before, that he hopes no one ever will again because he hates it, and that he's not about to retain Don.

Ah, what might have been. Just think what a little research could have done. A call from Don's secretary before the meeting. A couple of premeeting calls from Don to Barry's colleagues. A simple question from Don to Barry at the beginning of the meeting. But no, Don opted to trust his instincts and sally forth…into a "bear" trap.

The cost of not knowing

In Don's case, the cost of ignorance was a missed opportunity to win a client. When it comes to communications initiatives, the stakes are a lot higher. One out-of-focus ad, brochure, video or TV spot can result in hundreds of thousands of wasted production and media dollars.

What makes more sense: investing $75,000 and six weeks to know or rolling the dice, taking a chance with media and production expenditures that may be six times greater?

To ask the question is to answer it. When it comes to communications planning, the adages, "Ignorance is bliss" and "It pays to be ignorant," are about as far as you can get from the truth.

And yet many business people are reluctant to invest in research to buttress communications initiatives. Why do they hide behind the rationalizations I cited above?

• **Arrogance.** They really do think they already know.

*Warning: Out-of-date research is worse than useless. It's dangerous.

- **Apprehension.** They fear the time/money investment to get the facts will cost them more than going off half-cocked.
- **Professed impotence.** As captured in the cliche, "The train has already left the station; there's nothing I can do."

I wonder. Suppose the people who say this were to learn that the train was headed off a cliff and that their firstborn was on it. Do you think they'd still say, "There's nothing I can do"?

Sorry. As you can see, I don't have much sympathy for people who invent arguments for going off half-cocked. If you'll pardon the pun, I think it's cockeyed.

But what can you say to change their minds? How do communications people persuade arrogant, apprehensive, impotent colleagues who are itching to "get the word out" to invest the time and money necessary to make sure it's the right word?

An act of self-sabotage?

I liken building a communications initiative on cornerstones with fact gaps to building a bridge without checking the solidity of the ground it stands on, then worrying about its resistance to prevailing winds. Or, worse, designing time bombs into its stanchions.

A few suggestions

Tell horror stories. My story about Don, for instance. Stories that illustrate the high cost of guessing. If you don't know any, call any research director or supplier.

Use analogies. Construction analogies such as the bridge comparison in the sidebar above usually work pretty well. So do sports and warfare comparisons (depending on your audience). "You wouldn't send your team/army into a competition/ battle without first learning all you could about your opponent/enemy and the conditions of the playing/battlefield, would you? You'd be fired/hung in effigy/court martialed."

Ask provocative questions. "Do we know as much about our competitors' customers as our competitors know about ours?" "Do we know as much about our customers as our competitors do?" Or, most wickedly, "When was the last time we compared what our customers say *to* us with what they say *about* us?"

Appeal to their analytical instincts. If they're engineers, remind them that self-respecting engineers never attempt to solve a problem until they have an impeccable definition of it. If they're financial types, ask them what the finance professors they admired in graduate school would say about a financial model built on best guesses.

Point to stars in other industries. "P&G never stops doing this sort of research, you know." Or, "Coca-Cola starts researching prospects when they're in kindergarten." Or, "The best business-to-business companies, the Motorolas and Hewlett-Packards, wouldn't dream of launching communications initiatives that weren't based on rock-solid research."

Talk about the value of communications research beyond communications. "Imagine what our sales force could do with a study that told them how our customers regard our offerings vis-à-vis our rivals." Or, "Imagine how terrific it would be to have a study on the shelf that we could easily repeat every year or so to get a fix on the progress we're making."

Persuade a research company to put together a "spec" proposal. This can be particularly effective if it includes a prototypical questionnaire, which will give your doubting Thomases a palpable sense of what they will get in return for the time and money you're asking for.

Acknowledge two limits. First, all your colleagues can realistically expect from a single study is a snapshot of the market at a single moment. If they want to be able to spot trends, anomalies and discontinuities, you have to repeat it. (This, of course, is why political pollsters never stop polling once their campaigns get underway — and isn't that a scary thought?)

Second, even the most enthusiastic survey respondent can't tell you what he or she isn't consciously aware of. So, with one exception that I'll get to in a minute, research is hard-pressed to illuminate unperceived desires and genuine emotional reactions.

(For example, at the same time focus-group participants in a test market were railing about a particular product's "awful" advertising, their neighbors were buying so much of it that retailers couldn't keep it in stock.)

Acknowledge drawbacks. Not only is research no cure-all, a lot of it is at best useless, at worst counterproductive. Skeptics are right to be wary of the results. I divide research into "strategic" and "political." The former aims to get at what's really going on; the latter aims to support a point of view, enhance a relationship or provide cover for one's tail feathers.

Magazine surveys of their readers, for example, have to be scrutinized with care, as do all surveys that reveal their sponsor's identity to respondents. Mail surveys are suspect as are "omnibus" or "caravan" surveys, which sell questionnaire "shares" to multiple sponsors. (See below.)

What distinguishes strategic research? In a word, honesty. More specifically: robust sample sizes, careful questionnaire development, testing, a focus on statistically significant shifts, appropriate use of qualitative methods, alignment of expectations and methodology (e.g., don't expect people to reveal their attitudes toward African-American political candidates to a stranger over the phone).

So, is it wrong to call a dozen customers and ask them to react to alternative names for a new product you're planning to introduce? No. But neither is it research. You might get a useful insight or two, but you won't get a clue to how all the people you want to buy your new product will react.

Another drawback, one I've touched on earlier that's worth repeating: Questions must be written with great care and skill or their responses will lead you wildly astray. Great researchers are great questionnaire writers; it's the soul of the craft. The road to communications oblivion is paved with poorly written questions.

For example, a political poll found that "73 percent of whites agreed that Louis Farrakhan is anti-Semitic and bigoted against whites." This is a bear trap of a finding. Why? Because it doesn't tell you how many see him as anti-Semitic but not bigoted, or bigoted but not anti-Semitic. The questionnaire writer tried to find out two things with one question and wound up learning nothing.

The almighty focus group

When I started buying research, people looked down their noses at focus groups. Those who used them were called "grave robbers" (because they "spied" on participants from behind one-way mirrors).

Today they're used in darn near every situation, often inappropriately. Focus groups are an excellent way to jump-start the creative process, for example, and a lousy way to judge the results of this process.

Rule of thumb: Use focus groups when you're looking for ideas from your target audience; use one-on-one surveys when you're looking for reactions.

And the lambs will lie down with the lions

Traditionally, communications managers have dealt with research and creative people as Henry Kissinger dealt with Arabs and Israelis: discretely (and discreetly). They've done this because copywriters and art directors have typically seen researchers as wet blankets who could be counted on to smother ingenious inspirations with arcane statistics.

But a light is dawning. Perceptive writers and art directors have figured out that it makes more sense to work with researchers than it does to lob grenades at them. They've discovered that writers, art directors and researchers are natural allies for two reasons.

First, researchers can deliver insights that make it more likely that writers and art directors will be able to create communications that get heard. Second, researchers can figure out how to get answers to questions art directors and writers are anxious to ask.

I like to brainstorm with researchers every step of the way, but particularly at the start of their planning process. I want to think with them about their methods and react to their questionnaires. I defer to them, of course. I appreciate that what they do requires special expertise and sensitivity. But trading ideas with them inevitably results in my getting information I wouldn't have gotten otherwise, information I can use to fine-tune a plan, sharpen a message or dream up a great new strategy.

Moral: If you really want a first-rate research study, make sure you invite your creative people and your researchers to your planning table. While you're at it, you might want to invite your media, merchandising and sales promotion folks for good measure.

Strengths and weaknesses

Now let's look at the key strengths and weaknesses of specific research techniques.

Telephone surveys. Strengths: cost- and time-effective; deliver statistically significant findings; samples can be representative; anonymity can be preserved. Weaknesses: respondents won't divulge true feelings about sensitive issues; respondents' participation is often reluctant and/or desultory, especially if interviews run longer than 15 minutes.

Personal surveys. Strength: best way to obtain hard-to-get information. Weakness: expensive in terms of time as well as money.

Mail surveys. Strength: cheap. Weaknesses: unreliable because the sample isn't representative, no matter how large it is. The minority who respond (20 to 40 percent) are fundamentally different from the majority who don't.

Mall intercepts. Strength: speed. Weakness: unrepresentative samples; inadequate sample sizes; inability to deliver unaided, "top-of-mind" responses.

Psychological probes. Strength: produce in-depth information, including "between the lines" (subconscious) emotional responses. Weaknesses: expensive; unrepresentative samples.

Focus groups. Strengths: fast; produce insights that can inspire strategists. Weaknesses: often misused as a measurement device; participants tend to follow vociferous leaders instead of revealing personal thoughts and feelings; now so popular and so publicized that participants may play games.

Observational research. That is, research that employs social science techniques to study target audience behavior. Strength: By paying attention to how people live rather than what they say, it can produce profound insights that can lead to "breakthrough" products, services, communications, even businesses. Weaknesses: expensive in time and money terms; hard to find qualified researchers; susceptible to misinterpretation.

Which is most appropriate? It depends on what you want to know, what "fact gaps" you want to fill. But one thing is sure: Any one of them is more appropriate than flying blind.

It's too bad we can't compute the cost of ignorance as easily as the cost of research. Our jobs would be easier, our work would be better and our enterprises would be more successful.

Ten steps to reliable research

1. Write down what you want to learn.
2. Determine the appropriate methodology.
3. Define samples and determine how to validate them.
4. Write the questionnaire.
5. Test it (20 interviews).
6. Rewrite the questionnaire.
7. Repeat testing and rewriting until the questionnaire has been cleansed of all ambiguities.
8. Conduct the survey.
9. Study "top-line" results to determine analytical techniques and formats.
10. Analyze data; report findings.

Something for your pocket

Here are seven succinct arguments for "fact gap" research, designed to be used in hallway meetings:

- It takes a lot of the guesswork out of communications planning; firms up the situation and the cornerstones.
- It enables planners to reconcile differences without anyone having to "pull rank."
- It provides a yardstick with which to measure progress.
- It helps creative, merchandising, sales promotion and media people be more effective.
- It helps everybody avoid bear traps. The more you know, the less likely you are to say the wrong thing.
- It can point people in directions that never would have occurred to them otherwise.
- The more you do it, the more useful it is to do it. You get better at it and you have a richer context against which to measure current findings.

Chapter 9

The Heart of the Matter

Executive Summary

Objective:

Make your arguments irresistible to your target audience.

Strategies:

(1) Marry the factual and the inspirational, the analytical and the artistic. Imagine ways to dramatize your arguments; i.e., make your case.

(2) To do this, conceive an idea or set of ideas that relates to your offering and gains and holds your target audience's attention for as long as it takes to communicate your arguments.

 If you do this well, your target audience will smile reflexively when they see your messages, they'll understand them instantly, and a voice in their heads will whisper, "Wow!"

 To do this well, you must:

 • Know your target audience intimately.

 • Know your offering inside and out.

 • Know what you're trying to achieve and how much time and money you have at your disposal.

 • Recognize that, to be successful, to get heard, you have to connect with your target audience on an emotional level.

 • Recognize that "spin" (dubious, slippery finesses) doesn't connect. It has an unmistakable, unappealing aroma. Be real or be quiet.

 • Recognize that you have to resist the almost irresistible temptation to shout.

(3) The first step on the path to "Wow!" is to empathize with your target audience. Get on their wavelength. See the world and your offering through their eyes.

(4) The next step is to free-associate, with your target audience as your point of departure. Brainstorm till you come up with the idea(s) you're looking for.

These ideas will project the arguments in ways the target audience "gets" (as in gets a joke) and responds to. They will involve your target audience, engage them and foster a dialogue with them.

(5) Once your ideas are in hand and your presentation is taking shape, weave in relevant (to the target audience) human-interest stories and anecdotes if possible.

(6) Include demonstrations wherever possible to add to your communication's believability.

(7) Now that you think your communications are as electrifying as a Stephen King thriller and as unimpeachable as a Gallup poll, see what your target audience thinks. Test them. And revise as warranted.

"My kingdom for an idea!"

You've set the cornerstones. Now it's time to build the house.

You've determined the who, what, when and why of your communications initiative. Now you're ready to focus on the "how" and "where" of it; that is, how and where you present your arguments — make your case.

In this chapter and the four that follow it, we'll examine the "heart of the matter," the shape of your communications (words, pictures, style, voice). In chapter 14, we'll talk about delivery vehicles.

For the moment, imagine that you're a lawyer who's scheduled to argue before the U.S. Supreme Court in a month. You've done your research. You've buttoned down your case. Your task now is to come up with a way to present it that knocks the socks off the nine wise men and women on the bench (your target audience).

Art, meet science

Until now, we've focused on fact-gathering and analysis. We've laid solid cornerstones atop well-prepared ground. Step by step. With discipline and focus.

Now it's time to dream. Time to marry the factual and the inspirational, the analytical and the artistic. Time to imagine ways to dramatize your arguments, breathe energy and vitality into them. Make them interesting, compelling, memorable, persuasive, irresistible.

Your task is to dream up an idea or a set of ideas that relates to your offering and gains and holds your target audience's attention for as long as it takes to make your case. Naturally, the more unusual the ideas the better, as long as they aren't gratuitous.

If you imagine well, your target audiences will smile reflexively when they see your communications, they'll get your message instantly, and a voice in their heads will whisper, "Wow!"

They'll be glad they heard you.

Example: An ad for Porsche's four-wheel-drive sports car whose claim to fame is its road-holding tenacity. How does one communicate "road-holding tenacity" (the argument) to the doctors, lawyers, athletes, entertainers and business execs who might buy this car?

The admakers' answer was to relate it to peanut butter. The ad showed a lovely photo of the car snaking around a corner; it was captioned, "Like peanut butter to the roof of your mouth."

What a great idea! It communicated the argument/appeal instantly in a way that everyone in the target audience could relate to. Wow!

Can you see the tuning fork?

How do you trigger "wow!'s"? Start with who and what you know. First, you know your target audience. You know who they are, what makes them tick and what sorts of ideas are apt to catch their fancy.

You know the music they favor, the books they read (or don't read), the things that prompt them to do double takes. And you know what they're looking for from your offering — their "hot buttons."

Second, you know your offering, inside and out, features, benefits, points of distinction, arguments (a.k.a. seductive appeals.)

Finally, you know what you're trying to achieve with your communications initiative and how much time and money you have.

Now all you have to do is *dramatize* the appeals to the target audience in ways that achieve your objective within your budget and time frame. Pretty straightforward, eh?

Yes and no. A little prep work is required, a slight adjustment in your head. First, you have to convince yourself that the communications you're about to create are fundamentally different from those you typically author to friends and coworkers.

A brochure is not a memo. A speech is not a conversation.

In a memo or conversation, you say what you want to say and your correspondent reads/hears and acknowledges it. You can be pretty sure communication has "taken place," to use G.B. Shaw's term.

Unfortunately, when you're creating a brochure or speech, your saying what you want to say doesn't guarantee that your audience will hear it, no matter how elegantly precise and articulate you are.

You can't simply hand over the information like a quarterback hands off a football. You first have to predispose your audience to take what you hand them.

Picture a tuning fork. You strike one tine, it begins to vibrate, and pretty soon the other tine does, too. Effective communications are like the first tine. They connect. Their look, rhythm and tone prompt their audiences (the second tine) to feel "sympathetic vibrations."

"Only connect!"

Word for word, this is the greatest sentence ever written in English, in my humble opinion. E.F. Forster has his protagonist say it to her husband in the novel *Howards End*. She's urging him to get in touch with his feelings. I borrow it here to make a similar point.

Your communications must connect with your target audience on a visceral level before they can begin to work for you. *The New York Times* defines "connecting" as "touching readers' emotions." I define it as "triggering emotional responses that are beyond conscious control, a smile, a grin, a laugh, a tear, a memory, goosebumps, the aforementioned 'Wow!'."

I don't like musts, but here is one, at least as far as I'm concerned: You *must* make an emotional connection with your audience (even if — nay, especially if — your audience is the U.S. Supreme Court). It's this connection that separates effective communications from the also-rans.

Once you understand this, at a gut level, you're halfway home. You've just one more adjustment to make before you start imagining. You have to squelch, suppress, deep six, terminate with extreme prejudice the almost irresistible temptation to shout.

"Viva la revolucion!"

We're living and working at a time when a communications revolution is well underway. Media and "empowering" technologies proliferate. And a whole lot of money spent on communications is wasted.

The people we want to reach have more information sources than ever (check their in-, e- and voice-mail boxes, pagers and bedside tables), as well as the technological wherewithal to stuff rags in our mouths. Getting heard gets harder every day.

Which leads me to another must (sorry): We *must* avoid the presumption that our target audiences can't wait to hear what we have to say ("If we say it, they will listen"). We dare not pontificate, boast or bore. Above all, we must not shout.

When you're one of many who aim to attract the attention of time-constrained, info-loaded people who aren't inclined to listen, "Hey, you!" doesn't work. Jumping up and down and yelling louder is tempting, and it may make you feel better, but it seldom wins listeners.

So what's a communicator to do? How do we break through and get heard above the din? How do sellers attract and persuade buyers amid the cacophony — be they buyers of products, services, stocks, brands or viewpoints? Answer: Speak with a distinctive, empathetic, involving, engaging voice.

A good way to win listeners when everyone else is jumping up and down and yelling is to whisper.

Empathize, involve, engage

Imagine that you're trying to sell your car. It's an '89 Dodge sedan, so the phone isn't exactly ringing off the hook in response to your classified ad. But one night you get a call — a live one! You make a date to show off Old Reliable. When the prospect arrives, what do you do?

My hunch is that once you've introduced yourself, you'll begin to ask a few questions, gently, to get a sense of what sort of person you're dealing with and what the prospect is looking for in the way of a car.

You'll *empathize* so that you can get on your prospect's wavelength, speak your prospect's language…so you can wax poetic about Old Reliable in ways and words that are relevant to the potential new owner.

You may dial up or down, be sober-sided and understated or witty and garrulous. You may relate a few personal experiences. Or talk golf. Who knows? You won't decide until you know something about the person you're counting on to relieve you of your Dodge.

One thing's sure, though. Your communications will be interactive — you'll *involve* your prospect, *engage* him/her in a dialogue about things that matter to him/her on a gut level.

Gear shift. Carrot stick

Empathize, involve, engage. These are the keys to connecting on an emotional level (and hence getting heard) in these revolutionary times. As Benjamin Franklin said at another revolutionary time: "Tell me, and I'll forget. Show me, and I may remember. Involve me, and I'll understand."

So you're on the trail of an idea, or set of ideas, that will connect with your target audience, will engage and involve them, capture their fancy. These ideas are the heart of your communication. How do you find them?

As I mentioned in chapter two, the classic method is free association. That is, I say "gear shift," you respond by saying whatever comes to mind, then I say whatever comes to mind, etc. For example:

Me: "Gear shift."

You: "Carrot stick."

Me: "Eyesight."

You: "Eagle."

Persist, and eventually someone will say something that causes you to say "Aha!" or "Eureka!" because you'll have an idea that embodies and projects the point you're trying to make in a way that your target audience will "get" (as in getting a joke) and respond to.

Example: During the United States' confrontation with Iraq's Saddam Hussein in September 1996, the British newsweekly *The Economist* editorialized about U.S. foreign policy. The editors wanted to make the point that many nations saw U.S. foreign policy as potentially powerful, but inconsistent and unpredictable — "now you see it, now you don't."

To find an involving way to dramatize this point (I imagine), the editors got together and free-associated. "What will our readers relate to?" they asked. Holly Golightly? Politicians? The weather in the Himalayas? And then one editor, empathizing with the magazine's politically sophisticated readers, said, "How about the U.S. Air Force's Stealth bomber?"

"Eureka!" said his colleagues (I guess). "Our readers are well aware of the controversy surrounding the plane's production, its radar-evading capabilities and its use in last week's dust-up, so they'll quickly connect with your Stealth-as-symbol idea."

They'll "get it," in other words.

Given this idea, the editorial writer wrapped the prose around the plane-as-metaphor, and the art director used an eye-catching photo of the plane not only above the editorial, but also on the cover. The title of the "leader" (as *The Economist* labels its editorials): "Leadership by Stealth."

The departure point

Note the editors' point of departure: "What will our readers relate to?" This is where your free associations ought to start — with your target audience. You know what you want to say (others see U.S. foreign policy as hard to follow). What symbols, analogies or metaphors will involve and engage your audience?

Be patient

You may be able to knock out a memo or letter in an hour or two, but conceiving the ideas at the heart of your communications will probably take longer — like a week or two. Ideas grow. They need time to percolate. Rumination is usually a prerequisite for inspiration.

As is discipline. Ideas don't grow easily. Concentration is required. The artist who sits in a lounge chair in her back yard isn't watching the grass grow. She's working. Thinking. Musing. Brainstorming. Free-associating.

Team up

You'll probably find that the ideas will be better and come faster if you find a co-author or two to brainstorm with. Just remember three things:

- There's no such thing as a bad idea; your shopworn notion may inspire a partner to brilliance.

- There's no such thing as an irrelevant idea; your partner's off-the-wall idea may prompt you to come up with one that is out of the ballpark.
- Great ideas rarely have single parents. They tend to take shape through a series of genuinely spontaneous free associations among groups of uninhibited people… over time.

Lemonade out of nothing

What do you say about an offering that has nothing to say for itself, nothing to recommend it?

A Texas-based company buys a plant in California's High Desert country that sits in one corner of a 960-acre lot, and its executives instruct the plant manager to get rid of the "excess" acreage, which amounts to 950 of the 960.

The plant manager, who lives in the area, knows that people aren't exactly lining up to buy 950 acres of High Desert at any price, and decides that he'll do better by his new bosses if he turns the property into an industrial park and then sells it piece by piece to companies looking to set up distribution facilities.

To help him, he puts together a team that includes a landscape architect, a civil engineer, a lawyer/lobbyist, a commercial Realtor and a marketer (yours truly). We quickly determine that there is a market for industrial park space, but that our would-be industrial park has nothing to recommend it over others in the area. Conclusion: We have a once-in-a-professional-lifetime opportunity.

We can literally create something out of nothing. We have a 950-acre canvas with nothing on it (save sagebrush and empty beer and soda cans) upon which we can paint the industrial park of our dreams, a "workers' paradise."

This insight (or idea) leads directly to a communications strategy: Present the park to prospective companies not as it is today, but as we envision it a decade hence. To do this, we produce a combination live-action computer-animation video that invites viewers to travel forward in time and watch a workers' paradise take shape.

Happy result: Heroic California plant manager gets Texas execs out from under an albatross in a way that makes them money.

Tell stories

Some psychologists (they call themselves "evolutionary psychologists") maintain that our curiosity about our fellow humans is genetic, a survival mechanism designed to keep us alert to the possibility that someone out there might want to do us in. They give Darwin a gentle twist, argue that people who aren't curious aren't fit and won't survive.

(So the nosier we are, the better our chances.)

Whether they're right or wrong, it's certainly true that just about all of us are interested in, if not nosy about, our fellow human beings. Hence, the term "human interest." This being the case, communications that tell human-interest stories their target audiences identify with tend to get heard.

Good journalists do this to great effect. A *Wall Street Journal* article on anti-missile missiles, for example, will start by recounting Jane Smith's dream about bows and arrows. We'll soon learn, of course, that Ms. Smith lives next door to a planned missile site.

We all enjoy human-interest stories, if only because we're all human. They personalize our communications and connect us with our audiences.

Incidentally, don't be reluctant to tell stories about yourself. Personal experiences can make your anecdotes especially compelling.

Eschew spin

The term comes from the world of politics, as you know. "Spinmeisters" or "spin doctors" are supposed to invent positive interpretations of their employers' pronouncements and activities, and then communicate (i.e., sell) these interpretations to journalists and the public.

Today, many communications people (a few of whom toil in political vineyards) hold that the best spin is no spin. They prefer candor, not for high-minded moral reasons, but simply because there are now so many people investigating everyone's every move that finesses and machinations are likely to be exposed.

Technology, in the service of our aforementioned genetic curiosity, has midwived a rabbit-like proliferation of news media. Not that long ago, most communications moguls pronounced Ted Turner crazy for launching a worldwide, 24-hour, all-news TV channel. Now they're rushing to follow suit. Not just on TV, but on the Internet as well.

It's hard to keep secrets. So why try? Forgo image polishing ("spinning"). Focus instead on communicating your organization's character. Level with your target audiences. Be real. If you goofed, say, "We goofed." Nobody's perfect. Imperfections can be attractive.

Show your target audiences who you are and what you're made of — with actions as well as words. Demonstrate why you're proud to be a part of your organization. Just be sure to do it in ways they will relate to.

Subtle point ahead

When you show off your organization's character in your communications, you'll probably include information that doesn't relate directly to your target audience's interests (hot buttons). So how you express it becomes especially important.

The key, of course, is to couch what you want to say in their terms. Ask yourself, What do we know that our target audiences would find useful if they knew it, and how can we deliver this information in clear and interesting ways? If you can respond to yourself with real substance ("pearls," "gems," "news you can use"), you have the makings of a powerful communications initiative.

Incidentally, stories that make someone laugh at the end of a busy day are gems. Just make sure your target audiences think they're funny.

Actions speak more persuasively

U.S. submariners have an expression: "Watch their feet, not their lips." If this strikes you as good advice, then you, too, are an "I'm from Missouri; show me" skeptic like most of the rest of us, almost certainly including your target audience.

We live in a noisy, hype-filled era when the adage "Talk is cheap" is more widely believed than ever. Which means, as honest and decent and trustworthy as you and your organization are, your target audience is no more inclined to believe you than they are to listen to you in the first place. Their eyes are on your feet.

So dance. That is, turn your communications into demonstrations. Don't claim innovativeness. *Be* innovative. Demonstrate it. Example: A forest products company, intent on persuading opinion leaders that its logging and manufacturing operations are responsibly managed, runs ads that offer plant and logging site tours to the public in magazines read by opinion leaders.

Speaking of demonstrations, this campaign, which was quite successful, demonstrated anew journalist Theodore White's law of unintended consequences. To everyone's surprise, the people who responded most enthusiastically were the company's employees. They liked the campaign because it gave them a chance to show off their workplaces.

Incidentally, the ads themselves provide a good illustration of the free association process. Their authors brainstormed their way from plant tours to family outings to theme parks to Disneyland to "Magic Kingdom" to Merlin the magician. The ads featured dramatic illustrations of Merlin replanting forests and turning trees into wood and paper products before the eyes of two rapt youngsters. Captions read: "Show your kids how paper is made," "Show your kids how 2x4s are made" and "Show your kids how a forest is logged." A nice way to dramatize the argument, don't you think?

Surprise!

When his kids would break into tears, a writer I know would give them a hug, look them in the eye and whisper, "Don't laugh." They were so taken aback that they usually stopped crying...and often started laughing.

Moral: Surprise is good. Surprising your target audiences — offering the unexpected — is a good way to capture their attention, leapfrog their skepticism and hold their interest long enough to make your case.

Man bites dog

Have you seen this TV ad? Scene #1: a long shot of a tow truck and a car on the side of a road, back to back. Scene #2: a close-up shot of a tow truck driver taking the hook from the truck and securing it under the rear bumper of the car. Scene #3: another long shot of the car towing the truck down the road.

Or this one? Scene #1: three attractive women in nurses' outfits in a hospital setting. All carry cans of Pepsi Cola. Scene #2: they enter a room full of newborn babies and ogle one. Scene #3: a shot of the nurses ostensibly from the baby's perspective, fuzzy at first, then clearing to reveal one nurse smiling winsomely and mouthing the words, "I love you." Her Pepsi can is clearly visible. Scene #4: a close-up of the baby, who winks and puckers his lips. A graphic appears under his face: Norman Smith, Pepsi drinker for life.

These ads are effective because they surprise us, in the first instance by taking advantage of an image we all carry around with us, that of a tow truck towing a car, and in the second instance by presenting an image we can't imagine seeing, that of a newborn blowing a kiss.

However you create it, surprise is a powerful communications device — an attention grabber and holder. Try it and see.

Get ready to listen

Today's target audiences are saying, "You want my ear? Tell me something I find interesting and be prepared to listen to my response."

In our hyperactive, interactive age, one-way communications are dodo birds, gone geese, non-starters. All successful communications are dialogues, by definition. They're conversations, even if they're data sheets or direct mail pieces. Target audiences expect you to make it easy for them to respond and to pay attention to them when they do.

God bless 'em! Dialogues are easier and richer than monologues, right? We communicators get feedback, and feedback is nourishing. It inspires us and adds to our understanding of our target audiences and hence our ability to communicate effectively with them.

Moral: When you're creating your communications, make sure you design in a feedback loop. In fact, why not spend time free-associating about what sort of feedback loop would be especially appealing to your target audience?

Is your boss an E.F. Hutton?

The now-defunct E.F. Hutton brokerage firm ran a popular ad campaign a few years back that boasted, "When E.F. Hutton talks, people listen." Unfortunately, you can put many an executive's name in place of "E.F. Hutton," and improve the statement's accuracy. These are men (and, very occasionally, women) who believe that they command attention, that their various constituents strain to hear their every word.

Fortunately, they're dying off. The fact is, even the mightiest executive isn't listened to automatically. I can think of only a handful of people who are, and they all have essentially the same job. They head up their nations' central banks, and they don't want to be listened to. They generally aim not to communicate, but to obfuscate. What a paradox!

If you have E.F. Hutton-types in your organization, loan them this book, opened to this page.

Face it: Art is subjective

One person's magnificent conception is another's fish wrap. Some people yawn while looking at Michelangelo's Pieta, prefer "Texas Chainsaw Massacre" to "Casablanca" and like broccoli.

While most of us will agree that art moves people (and so, the more artful your communications, the better), rare indeed is the single *objet d'art* that moves everybody. So be prepared to defend yours. (I'll discuss how in chapter 17.)

What matters, of course, is how effectively your artistry moves your target audience and how consistent it is with your organization's personality.

You can test the first. The second is a Bermuda Triangle in disguise. If you're not careful, debates about the style of your communications can paralyze your team and, perhaps, your organization. ("We're not doing anything until we can do something everybody can live with.")

This leads to what I call the "Ninth Wave" phenomenon. You may remember that Eugene Burdick wrote a novel by this title about a surfer who sets out at dawn in search of the perfect wave and returns at sunset without ever having ridden a single wave. He let every wave go by because he thought the one behind it might be better.

The way out of this conundrum is to experiment. Do some one-on-one research or test a couple of approaches in different markets. Whatever happens, you'll learn something. Communications are organic. They're meant to grow and change and improve and teach. The more we do it, the better we'll be at it.

How do you talk to people who won't listen to you?

The assignment seemed straightforward: "We want to convince the citizens of our state to give greater support to our public schools." Trouble was, as we quickly discovered when we started in on our situation analysis, the citizens saw public education as a perpetual motion vacuum cleaner that did nothing but suck tax dollars from their purses and wallets. The instant they heard or saw the words "public schools" or "public education," they tuned out. Minds closed.

So it was that our first order of business was to come up with a communications strategy that would pry open those closed minds. Otherwise, there was no point in investing nickel one in communications. Our solution was to talk with our target audience about a related subject that all of them were open-minded about: children. The theme of our communications initiative was, "Love kids," and it featured specific things people could do to help kids in their communities, one of which was to get involved in their communities' public schools.

The messages also highlighted a new community organization set up expressly to help kids and invited people to participate in its activities, many of which were school or education-based.

Moral: Don't beat your head against the wall; find — or invent — a way around it.

On another occasion, we ran into a wall that successfully resisted all of our efforts to imagine a way around it. The subject: automobile insurance. The sponsor: a coalition of insurance companies. The objective: persuade citizens to lobby for auto insurance reform legislation. The wall: as far as the citizenry was concerned, auto insurers were sleazeball, scumbag rip-off artists.

Naturally, the auto insurers' view, which we were supposed to communicate, was rather different. They saw themselves not as villains, but as victims caught in an unholy web of car thieves, uninsured drivers, rings of doctors, lawyers and body shop operators who staged accidents, then filed (and, if necessary, sued for) egregious medical claims on behalf of the "victims."

The auto insurers had the facts on their side, but all the facts in the world seemed useless in the face of the target audience's towering rage.

But when we conducted focus group interviews with our target audience to see if they'd show us a way through this wall of rage, we saw a fascinating phenomenon. Participants would invariably begin by blasting auto insurers, but once they had unburdened themselves, many were willing to acknowledge that uninsured drivers, thieves and professional swindlers did contribute to their sky-high rates.

This behavior pattern led to a three-step communications strategy. First, acknowledge the rage (thereby demonstrating that auto insurers are neither insensitive nor hard of hearing). Second, cite disinterested third-party data to document the real reasons behind the high costs. Third, invite public scrutiny and offer convenient opportunities to sound off to auto insurers, either personally or electronically.

We ran ads that featured real people sounding off, mailed personal letters, hosted call-ins and put on forums, and an interesting thing happened: Target audience members began to redirect their rage and to lobby for reforms the auto insurers supported — which, as you recall, was the initiative's objective.

Moral: Sometimes simply acknowledging a wall is the best way over it.

Yesterday, today and tomorrow

The chart below contrasts yesterday's communications orthodoxies with what I think tomorrow's will be. As you look it over, you might find it helpful to see it as a spectrum and ask yourself where your organization's communications are on it.

You might also want to use the items in the right column as a checklist against which to measure your organization's communications.

Yesterday	Tomorrow
Aims to be admired	Aims to do admirable things
Touts	Acts in ways that prompt others to tout
Polishes image	Expresses character
Claims	Demonstrates
Talks features	Talks benefits
Hypes	Understates
Gee whiz!	So what?
Pronounces	Involves/engages
Explicates	Converses
One-way	Multi-way
Institutional	Personal/human
Sells	Informs (to sell)
Thinks Montaigne is a wine	Knows Montaigne said, "A word is half his who speaks it, half his who hears it."

Chapter 10

Magic Words

Executive Summary

Objective:

Produce copy that your target audience finds irresistible.

Strategies:

(1) Empathize. Understand that the people you're writing to:
  - Don't have time to read what they want to read, much less what you want them to read.
  - Headline hop, subheadline hop, check captions and special offers.
  - Are probably doing something else while they're reading.
  - Are from Missouri ("I'm from Missouri, show me").

(2) Thus your writing must:
  - Get to the point, quickly and succinctly.
  - Connect emotionally.
  - Be specific.
  - Be straight.
  - Use words your audience understands.

(3) Start with "you." It puts you on your target audience's wavelength, says you're going to deal with things that matter to them.

(4) Let your facts speak. Don't exaggerate.

(5) Try candor and truth. They're unexpected, therefore disarming.

(6) Steer clear of:
  - "We" (self-interested, reader-unfriendly)
  - Words that ring hollow ("friend")
  - Subjective words ("quality")
  - Hype ("exciting")

- Weasel words ("virtually")
- Buzzwords ("world class")
- The passive voice
- Euphemisms
- Boilerplate
- Unfunny funnies

(7) Make sure your copy is structured — *head* (attention-getting lead) followed by *body* (makes the case) and *close* (spells out desired actions, "tell a friend").

(8) Choose from five kinds of heads: *provocative, news, promise, command, selective.* Your criterion: appropriateness.

(9) Choose from three copy styles: *reason why* (fact-oriented), *human interest* (anecdotal, emotional), *combination.*

(10) Think visually (see your story in pictures, write captions).

(11) Think dialogue (all communications are two-way today).

(12) Don't forget taste and class. Talk up, not down, to your target audience.

(13) Don't forget that 10 people read headlines for every one who reads body copy.

(14) Remember, there are only three hard and fast rules:

- Thou shalt not bore.
- Thy words shall be appropriate given the situation and cornerstones.
- Thou shalt communicate unto others as thou wouldst have others communicate unto thee.

"Sexist!" "But true."

Caution: We're about to separate the inseparable.

In fact, a speech, brochure, video, ad or Web site is a single entity comprised of components that, ideally, fit perfectly together — words, pictures, logos, addresses, slogans, sounds, et. al.

Take the Porsche ad I mentioned in chapter nine: Words, pictures and layout (design) mesh so neatly that, if you took away one, you'd have nothing.

Nonetheless, the laws of linearity being as they are, I'll discuss words in this chapter and visualization and layout in the next. Please be aware, though, that the distinction is artificial. Communications are like the engine in your car. If all the parts aren't in place and in sync, you're not going anywhere.

And now…on to what is, arguably, the key part of almost every communication, the spark plug, if you will: words. Your chances of creating communications that your target audience finds irresistible are incomparably greater if your words are irresistible.

So how to write irresistible words?

First, empathize

Climb into your target audience's collective head and you come face to face with a few unpleasant facts of life:

- You're writing to people who don't have time to read what they want to read, much less what you want them to read. (Or watch what they want to watch. Or listen to what they want to listen to.)

  Which means, if you're not careful, you'll experience every writer's worst nightmare: Our magnificent words go unread. We have labored mightily to produce nothing.

- You're writing to people who, when they do read, don't do it the way their parents did — from beginning to end. They read selectively, headline hop, subheadline hop, check out the offer at the end, the captions.

- You're writing to people who are typically doing something else at the same time they're reading — eating, talking on the phone, watching TV, listening to the radio or brushing their teeth.

  The brothers who host National Public Radio's "Car Talk" complain often about people who read while driving. So you're probably not going to get your target audience's undivided attention. Do I have yours?

- You're writing to people who are genetically, biochemically skeptical. They, like you and I, have caught more than enough sales pitches to be exquisitely sensitive to the slightest whiff of bullfeathers.

Tips

- *Get to your point.* Say what you have to say quickly. Brevity is the soul of art. ("Sorry I wrote you such a long letter. I didn't have time to write a short one.")

- *Be clear.* Remember, you're not out to dazzle your target audience with your literary prowess. Comprehension is your goal.

- *Say it with feeling.* Chapter nine's tuning fork idea revisited. You aim to connect on an emotional level, so build some emotion into your message.

- *Be straight.* Ernest Hemingway said, "What every writer needs is a good BS detector." Today, just about every reader has two.

  Resist the impulse to overstate. Ask yourself, "If I were my audience, would I believe what I'm about to say?" Let your answer determine what you do.

  Rule of thumb: If you think they might not believe it, don't say it.

- *Be specific.* Generalities are quickly forgotten.

- *Forgo esoterica.* Speeches, brochures, ads are not good places to show off your vocabulary.

- *Communicate unto others as you would have them communicate unto you.* Think about how you react to communications directed at you; figure your target audiences will react the same way to messages you aim at them and communicate accordingly.

How to write great headlines

Many writers assume that because a headline will lead off their story, they have to write it first, and they struggle to find that marvelously pithy combination of words that dramatically captures the essence of their tale. They usually fall short.

They fall short because they haven't thought through their story, haven't done the hard thinking that takes place only as we reduce our stories to writing, put words on paper.

Your chances for headline immortality ("Ford to NY: Drop Dead") get a whole lot better when you write your headlines last. You'll typically discover them in your stories' third or fourth paragraphs.

And great copy

If your headline is hiding in your third paragraph, you'll want to ask yourself whether your story would be more compelling, more reader-friendly, if you jettisoned — or at least shortened — paragraphs one and two.

Are they in fact just a preamble, something you wrote to get your brain in gear, much as runners run a few laps before they get to the starting line? If so, lose them. Your copy will be better for it.

The magic word

If words are spark plugs, this word is the generator. It's how you get your time-constrained, information-overloaded target audiences to hear you and believe you amid all the hype and clamor.

There are those who say that the most compelling words in the language are "free" and "new." But they're wrong. The most compelling word is "you."

"You" puts you on your target audience's wavelength. It says, "I'm going to talk about things that matter to you" (as opposed to "we," which says the opposite).

"You" signals your audience that you've heard them, walked in their shoes, are interested in and care about their concerns.

"You," followed by knowing references to your target audience's interests and their views of your offering, engages them.

If you're writing to investors, for example, you might well begin, *"You'd probably like to know more about how you can profit from our plans..."*

Or, suppose your audience consists of potential venture partners. You might begin, *"You have probably lived through co-development ventures, some good, some bad..."*

Last word about "you": If XYZ Inc. hired me to move the company's communications from the Yesterday column to the Tomorrow column (see page 86), the first thing I'd do is ask XYZ's information technology folks to program my writers' computers not to turn on until their users had entered Y-O-U.

As they refined their work, they might turn to other, more indirect ways to engage their target audiences — a relevant (to the audience) anecdote, for instance. But I'd know, if they started with Y-O-U, they would have gotten to it by walking in their audience's shoes.

Other turn-ons

Do you remember this?

Butch Cassidy has been challenged to a knife fight by a very large man who wants to take over the Hole-in-the-Wall Gang. He accepts, then says, "But first we have to agree on the rules." "Rules? In a knife fight?" the giant bellows, distracted. Whereupon Butch fells him with a well-placed sucker kick.

Or this?

Baltimore Joe and his posse have Butch and Sundance cornered. Their only hope is to jump off a cliff into a roaring river 75 or so feet below. It's a moment of high drama, but then, suddenly, improbably, as they're running toward the edge of the cliff, Sundance hollers, "I just remembered! I can't swim!"

I resurrect these golden oldies to illustrate a timeless principle. The scenes connect exceptionally well with their audiences because they trigger conflicting emotions simultaneously. You laugh and grip your armrests or bite your nails at the same time.

When you create a communication that does this, you've hit a grand slam.

Here are a few other turn-ons:

Let your facts speak. Instead of telling your target audience that your widget is great, give them the reasons for its greatness, and leave it at that.

As film director Stanley Kubrick observed, "No matter how you say it, when you say something directly, it's simply not as powerful as when you let people discover it for themselves."

Don't be afraid to understate. As I mentioned a chapter ago, when everybody else is yelling and screaming, a whisper stands out. It's a sign of your respect, and your target audience is certainly worthy of that. They buy your widgets, after all.

Try candor. It's usually unexpected, therefore disarming, and, potentially, winning. When you say to me, "We screwed up," you've broken through my defenses and opened my mind, at least provisionally, to what you have to say.

Try truth. Again, it has a ring to it, especially when others are gilding their lilies.

The No. 1 turnoff

Among words that disconnect, one merits special attention because it's especially powerful and ubiquitous. We're all inclined to use it whenever we have something we really want to tell our audiences. The word is "we."

"We" and its brethren, "our" and "us," forewarn audiences that what's coming concerns the writer; that is, it will likely be self-interested rather than interesting (to them), writer-friendly rather than reader-friendly.

"We're changing the world." "Our products are simply superior." "America looks to us for leadership."

And yet, how many communications have you seen that begin, "We…" or "Our…" or "To us…"?

Message to all who incline to use "we": Turn your story inside out. Start with "you." Tell your audiences what your good news can do for them.

Example: Which of these heads do you find more compelling?

- *We found a cure for cancer.*
- *Now you don't have to worry about cancer anymore.*

Suggestion: If you're absolutely stuck with "we," add a "how" or a "why" as in, *"How we found a cure for cancer."*

Sometimes the best sell is no sell

When you have a solid story to tell, it's often best to let your facts speak for themselves. Forgo the 21-gun salutes, forswear the adjectives and adverbs, and content yourself with communicating information. You'll be very persuasive.

The worst offenders

It may be because they have to deal with so many tense, irascible people, but airlines are especially prone to incredible, euphemistic, tone-deaf communications.

Gate agents and pilots seem oblivious to the skepticism and irritation that greet their lily-gilding pronouncements ("We should be pushing back in just another two or three minutes, folks"). And airline promotional writers are even worse. (An airline whose name, when scrambled, spells the state of most teenagers' shoes, recently sent its customers a high-minded "principles" booklet that promised "warm and genuine attention" and "frank answers and real solutions when you have problems." Hmmm. How about when they have problems?)

Can't they hear? Don't they understand how counterproductive these sorts of communications are? How anger-making? One day, some airline somewhere will discover the power of straight talk ("We're not sure when your flight will leave; we'll keep you informed"). I can't wait.

> ## Can competitors say it?
>
> A client once came up with a surefire way to keep us on our toes: He covered the signature of an ad we'd presented and asked if a competitor could run it.
>
> Your goal is copy that's so distinctive you could cover your signature and your target audience would still be able to identify the sponsor.

Other turnoffs

Has this ever happened to you?

Your flight is about to leave the gate — 54 minutes after the second officer announced a "minor problem that will take just a few minutes to fix" — when the gate agent comes on the PA system and says, "We'd like to apologize for the brief delay."

Brief? The word sticks in your craw.

In the air now, you attack your mail and come across a letter from an oil company trying to sell you mortgage insurance. The salutation reads, "Dear friend."

Friend?

The writers who chose these words have tin ears. They've failed to appreciate Michel de Montaigne's 500-year-old dictum, "A word is half his who speaks it, half his who hears it."

Here's a partial list of turnoff words, grouped by categories that sometimes overlap:

Words that are hollow. Like "friend." Even politicians are exorcising this one from their vocabulary.

Words that are hard to define objectively. Like "quality" or "beauty," as in "Our new Edsel is a thing of beauty."

Claims without support. I attended a Major League Baseball game this summer and counted 51 billboards, plus a "jumbotron" TV screen and a digital scoreboard that flashed sales pitches between innings. We are surrounded by hype and, as a consequence, disinclined to believe unsupported claims.

Adjectives whose aim is to hype. "Exciting," "wonderful," "spectacular," "terrific," "great," et. al.

Unsupported superlatives and comparatives. "Lowest rates in town" or "second to none," both of which are read or heard as, "Same as everybody else."

Weasel words. Like our old friend "briefly" or those old favorites, "very," "really," "virtually" and "significantly."

Buzzwords. "World class." "Our people." "Productivity enhancements."

Words like these are a tap on your target audience's collective knee. They trigger a reflexive disconnection, usually unconscious.

Still more turnoffs:

The passive voice. The choice of bureaucrats everywhere. "It was decided that…" "Mistakes were made…" By whom?

Euphemisms. Provide "warnings" instead of "advisories," and your target audience will be more accepting and attentive. Euphemisms are wet blankets. They make a communication "almost right," and that's an oxymoron. When it comes to communications, almost right is wrong.

Institutional boilerplate. Watch out for this stuff. It's in the memories of our organization's computers and, at the end of the day, it's tempting to drop a paragraph or two into a press release, stump speech or earnings report. No matter that these communications are to people, not institutions.

Please note: The aural equivalent of institutional boilerplate is public domain music. When your sound engineer suggests a few bars of "Unchained Melody" to spice up your corporate video, tout the virtues of a cold shower.

Special emphases. <u>Underlining</u>. Exclamation points! ALL CAPS. *Italics.* **Words in bold.** Seen as hype if not obviously warranted.

Sloppiness. Misspellings, mispronunciations, punctuation and grammatical mistakes (like "data is…" and "media is…"), factual inaccuracies, typos. They tell your audiences that you don't care.

The Great Northern Nekoosa paper company ran a full-page ad in business journals trumpeting its new name, which was spelled "Nekosa" in the body copy. Lucky for Great Northern that only about one in 10 ad readers get through the body copy.

The pre-eminent New York ad club, the One Club, ran a full-page ad in *The New York Times* that saluted the winners of its annual awards, one of whom was the author of Little Caesar's advertising…spelled "Caeser's" in the ad.

Unfunny funnies. As the author of Little Caesar's advertising has proved consistently, humor is a powerful communications device. If you try it, though, make sure you succeed.

Hitting bottom

Not long ago, I attended an annual meeting and subsequently received a transcript of the CEO's speech. The words "we," "our," "us," "me" and "I" appeared 178 times. The name of the company appeared 23 times. The words "you" and "your" appeared 10 times.

There were no anecdotes, no attempts to engage and involve the audience. It was an example of anti-communication, how to make darn sure no one listens. And he was speaking to his fellow stockholders, people who shared his interests and enthusiasms, people who were disposed to listen.

His loss can be your gain. Count the "we"s, "our"s and "you"s in your communications. If they're heavy on the first person and light on the second, rewrite. (For the record, I lifted this invaluable idea from an invaluable book, Rudolph Flesch's *The Art of Readable Writing,* published in 1943.)

Mechanics

Bear in mind two things when you aim to write irresistible copy: structure and style.

Whether you're writing a 30-second radio script or a 24-page capabilities book, there should be a structure to your copy that consists of *head* (or lead), *body* and *close*.

The *head* aims to attract your target audience's attention ("Pssst"). The *body* convinces them to act. The *close* tells them how to act.

Incidentally, the best leads not only stop your target audience, they also deliver your primary argument. Readers of the aforementioned Porsche ad who read only "Like peanut butter to the roof of your mouth" got its main point.

A thought starter

When you're crafting a communication, think "Here's how our offering helps you…" (the target audience), then present it in this context.

The five heads

When you're writing copy, you can select from a menu of five kinds of heads:

- Provocative ("Does she or doesn't she?").
- News ("Behold the world's first 100 mpg car").
- Promise ("One evening with Dermaglo and you'll feel young again!").
- Command ("Buy this, or else!").
- Selective ("If you're left-handed, listen up!").

Your choice will depend on your cornerstones — arguments, target audience, objective, budget and time frame. If you have a compelling argument and a diverse target audience, you'll probably write a telegraphic news head.

If, on the other hand, you're writing about a parity product to a selective audience that's familiar with it, you'll likely write a provocative head — to entice your audience into your story.

You might also mix and match. Some of the best heads are combinations. My favorite was penned more than a decade ago by my daughter, who was 9 at the time. She had agreed — most reluctantly — to travel with her mom to a small village in Mexico. Two days after she arrived, she sent me a letter that began, "The worst thing is the bugs." Your basic combination news/provocative head.

> Dear, Dad
> The worst thing is the Bugs!
> The squorpennis, cockroches and messcey toes. Whenever you get dressed you have to cheack your closes for bugs. But other—wise it's great! Romon and Baelin are the ones that make our breckfast. The make a good breckfast.
>
> Love, Abby

Copy style

There are three general copy styles: *reason why, human interest* and, you guessed it, a combination of the two.

Reason why tends to be crisp, telegraphic and used when your offering has a clear and compelling (to the target audience) competitive edge; e.g., a car that sticks to the road like peanut butter to the roof of your mouth.

Writers favor the more emotional *human interest* approach when their arguments aren't particularly compelling or when their target audiences aren't particularly interested in the product/service category (detergents, for example). The human-interest style is personal, anecdotal, narrative. "Mary Jones still remembers when she first heard the footsteps."

When writers mix the two, they typically lead with a human interest anecdote, then follow with the facts and figures:

Lead: Mary Jones still remembers when she first heard the footsteps.

Body: They convinced her once and for all to buy Hush Puppies because four separate Underwriter's Laboratory tests demonstrated conclusively that Hush Puppies, and only Hush Puppies, never make a sound no matter what you're walking on or how hard you're walking.

Regardless which you choose, remember, you're out to connect with your target audience on an emotional level. Somewhere along the line, you'll want to give your message a twist, perhaps visually, that does this.

It may seem paradoxical at first blush, but a reason why copy style lends itself to humor; e.g., "Six reasons to buy Dermaglo…" and three are spoofs. David Letterman uses a reason why style when he presents his top 10 lists. Johnny Carson was a master. Fact, fact, fact, twist. Fact, fact, fact, twist.

If you do this, just make sure your twists are as funny to your target audience as the great Carson's were to his.

Think visually

Another paradox: Some of the best writers are also excellent visual artists. They "see" pictures in their minds' eyes, then write captions. The grand master of this approach was, of course, James Thurber, who was nearly blind.

The idea is to write about what you see — in your mind's eye. Give it a try. Chances are, your words will be, if not irresistible, at least compelling.

Think dialogue

I made the point a chapter ago that, nowadays, even data sheets are two-way communications. Target audiences expect to be offered a mechanism that enables them to respond with minimal expenditures of time and money on their part.

This expectation now extends to the news media. Have you noticed? Newspapers, radio stations, even TV stations offer "talk back" numbers, Internet addresses and, occasionally, space or time for reader/listener comments.

My local newspaper, for example, publishes an "Other Voices" op-ed column that features the observations of our area's would-be pundits, who, needless to say, aren't paid for their punditry. (So they can retain their amateur status?)

Talk about dialogue. I wrote a letter to the editor of *The New York Times* recently and received replies from him and from the correspondent who wrote the article I commented on — and who was based in Sarajevo.

On another occasion, I faxed a letter to the editor of *The Economist* and received a return fax the same day.

In an environment like this, copy that's informal and conversational is most effective. Write as if you were engaged in a dialogue, and your target audience will likely do just that.

Don't forget taste and class

Did you see this?

A tequila distributor ran a four-page ad in national magazines that featured a series of color photographs of a beautiful woman in a two-piece beach outfit striding ever closer to the camera. Only on the final page is there copy. The headline, printed over the model's bra, reads, "She's a he." The subhead, strategically positioned at the model's crotch, reads, "Life is harsh. Your tequila shouldn't be."

Or this?

The left page of a two-page magazine ad for a video accelerator shows a glum fellow, naked except for a video display terminal that hides his private parts and displays a small fig leaf. On the right, we see the same fellow, still in his birthday suit, his privates covered by the same terminal, but smiling now, presumably because the fig leaf it displays is much larger. The caption: "Full-motion video accelerators. Yet another instance where size is everything."

I graduated from the "you catch more with honey" school, where I learned that classier is better, more tasteful is more effective. I think this so-called "in your face" communications style misses the mark, and I suggest that you avoid it.

It confuses "making an impact" with "making a positive impact." The objective of your communications isn't simply to grab your target audience's attention, it's to persuade them to think, feel or act in a particular way.

Are tequila drinkers more inclined to buy a particular tequila brand because it features a transvestite in its advertising? Do video accelerator buyers tilt toward a particular brand because it titillates them with a ribald *double entendre*?

Or, perhaps more appropriately, are there other, more tasteful (no pun intended) approaches that more tequila drinkers and video accelerator buyers would find more persuasive? To ask these questions is to answer them.

Contrast these "in your face" communications with this one. Thirty years ago, the British Travel Association ran an ad that featured a lovely photograph of Westminster Abbey's Henry VII chapel, a headline that invited readers to "Tread softly past the long, long sleep of kings" and 200 marvelously evocative words wooing them to visit Britain's cathedrals. Irresistible!

Be tasteful and classy. Talk up, not down, to your target audience. You won't regret it.

A tone setter

When you sit down to write your speech, press release, brochure or video, start by typing "Dear," add the name of a person you know who personifies your target audience and write a personal letter about your subject.

Think appropriateness

As you know, when it comes to writing, once you get past "Thou shalt not be boring" and "communicate unto others as you would have others communicate unto you," you've learned just about all the rules there are. We're talking art form here.

The key, of course, is to use ideas and techniques that are appropriate to your particular initiative, given your particular circumstances.

"Given what I know about my audience and my sponsor, how are they apt to react to what I've created? Will they think/feel/act as my sponsor wants them to?"

If the answer is yes, put down your pencil and take a break. You've earned it.

Naturals

As you may know, some of the best reporters in the world absolutely depend on editors and rewrite people to make their stories come to life. What they're good at is digging, coming up with the stuff of the story. If you can do that, you're a valuable part of your communications team, even if you're not F. Scott Fitzgerald.

F. Scott Fitzgeralds are born, not made. And rare, by definition. So if your deathless prose seems dead to you, don't feel bad. And don't kill yourself trying to bring it to life. Find yourself a good editor, rewrite person or ghost-writer, and get help.

You may find it where you least expect it. I've bought cigars from a mail order distributor for many years, in part because I love the catalog I get now and then. What can I say? The person who writes it has the touch. I read about things I have no interest in just for the words. Poetry. From a cigar distributor.

Chapter 11

Magic Pix

Executive Summary

Objective:

Create visual presentations your target audience finds irresistible. "Grabbers."

Strategies:

(1) Start at the beginning — with the business situation and cornerstones.

(2) Determine what sorts of visual images and design styles are most likely to appeal to your target audiences. (Note: Type is a visual image.)

(3) Brainstorm, free-associate with your colleagues to come up with an idea that dramatizes your arguments to your target audience in a way that promises to achieve your objective within your budget and time frame.

(4) Create visual representations of this idea (e.g., Michelin's baby in a tire; Absolut's bottle puns).

(5) Design your communication; that is, position its elements (visualization, lead, body, close, signature, sounds) relative to one another.

(6) Goals:

- Stopping power. Your communication prompts your target audience to stop whatever they're doing and consider your argument.

- Connecting power. It packs an artistic punch, connects with your target audience on an emotional level.

- Projecting power. It radiates your organization's character and personality.

(7) Yardsticks:

- How appealing is its shape (are its shapes) to your target audience?

- How well does its scale fit the tale?

- To what degree are the elements in balance, or proportion?

- How simple is it?

- How unerringly will it lead your target audience's eyes through your argument?
- How much warmth, honesty and humanity does it project?
- Does it pretend to be something it's not?
- How well will it wear?
- How pleasing to the eye is it?

(8)   Score your answers to these questions on a 1-10 scale. If they don't add up to at least 80, you don't have a grabber. Return to your drawing board.

"It's great all right, but is it art?"

Wrong question. The question to ask is:

"Will it grab 'em?"

Is the visual representation of your argument (a.k.a. appeal) so irresistible that your time-constrained, hype-resistant, information-overloaded target audience will stop whatever they're doing and pay attention to it?

Is it, in a word, a "grabber"?

If the answer is yes, you can ask your colleagues and yourself:

- Does it telegraph our primary argument?
- If not, does it lead our target audience to it quickly and surely?
- Does it make an emotional connection?
- Does it project our character and personality clearly and accurately?

As I'm sure you realize, it's almost impossible to overstate the importance of powerful visualizations when it comes to creating communications that get heard. Thanks to TV, film and the quest for a common language in our "global village," we live in an increasingly visual world.

Visual images dominate. The Berlin Wall. Challenger. Arafat and Rabin shaking hands. Michael Jordan flying. Pavarotti singing. Arnold Schwarzenegger strutting. British sociologist Kenneth Clark has said that film is the art form of the 20th century.

Today, only 59 percent of U.S. households receive a daily newspaper, and in perhaps one-third of them, only the sports, comics and TV pages get read regularly. Among Americans under 30, only three in 10 read a newspaper "regularly."

Of course (and fortunately for us), nearly all communications have visual components, even radio broadcasts, where one uses sound to create images inside listeners' heads (a la Orson Welles' "War of the Worlds").

If you're writing a speech, whoever will deliver it is a visual component, as are the visual aids she/he will use.

If you're creating a presentation to new employees, the visual components are your slides or foils, of course, as well as the person(s) who will speak to them.

Even an all-type "white paper" has visual components — the size, style and color of the type face you choose, the leading (space between lines), the margins, the number of columns, the color of the paper. (Have you noticed how often "white papers" are printed on gray, pearl or tan paper?)

The point, of course, is that your communications will almost certainly include a visual dimension that will affect, rather profoundly, how well they are heard. So it's essential to pay attention to it.

What makes for a grabber?

There are three interrelated ingredients:

- **Stopping power.** Grabbers disrupt, prompt their target audiences to stop whatever they're doing and consider the argument.

  Great Britain's Conservative Party published a poster that showed a demonized Labor Party leader with red dots in his eyes. The designer positioned the retouched photo so that the subject's eyes were centered just above the poster's midpoint (at "optical center," where your eye lands when you look at a printed piece). The eyes, with their tiny red dots, stared out at you. It was eerie. And riveting.

- **Connecting power.** Grabbers pack an artistic punch, the majesty of the Matterhorn or a panther in full stride; the beauty of an Eames chair or a Steuben vase; the vitality of a Picasso sketch.

  Whatever it is that triggers a tingle on the back of your neck, a reflexive smile or goosebumps on your arms, grabbers have it. They make an instant emotional connection with their target audiences. They're exciting.

- **Projecting power.** Grabbers radiate their sponsor's character and personality. Their target audiences don't have to check the logo to learn who the message is from. Grabbers carry another kind of signature.

As these ingredients suggest, grabbers are distinctive, by definition. They stand apart. You never ask yourself, "Have I seen this before?" "Is this a Dali or a Monet?" "Is this an ad for Mercedes or BMW?"

As important, grabbers are always telegraphic, never enigmatic. When you figure your target audience will decide whether to pay attention to your message in one-tenth of a second, you realize there's no time to be coy.

By the way, you don't need holographic photos of a panther in midair to create a grabber. In fact, you don't need any sort of picture. Type can grab.

Low-tech, high impact

To create a compelling audio-visual presentation you have to use a state-of-the-art computer software program, right?

Not necessarily. The most dramatic A/V presentation I've witnessed in years was decidedly low-tech, though very high on imagination.

The speaker was a computer scientist and his audience consisted of two dozen corporate information officers, so you had every reason to expect a high-tech show. But the presenter eschewed bells and whistles in favor of an overhead projector and a white board.

It's what he did with these antiques that made the presentation so dramatic and effective. He married them. He projected his foils onto his whiteboard, then used markers to draw on both. It was fascinating. First, he'd circle a number on a foil, then he'd walk to the whiteboard and draw an arrow from this number to another number.

It was akin to a football coach diagramming an exceedingly complicated play on a chalkboard (or a TV sports broadcaster making squiggles on our TV screens).

But he did something beyond the capacity of any TV sports announcer. He invited his audience to sketch along. He'd draw on a foil and the whiteboard, then offer his markers to anyone who wanted to embellish or debate the point he was making. Of course, once the picture became incomprehensibly messy, he'd simply erase and start over.

He had his audience in the palm of his hand and he demonstrated anew that, paraphrasing one of Einstein's great aphorisms, "Imagination is more important than knowledge" — or technology.

The process in a nutshell

If you're responsible for your communication's visual dimensions (visualization and design), start with a thorough understanding of the basics — business situation and cornerstones. You become intimately familiar with your target audience, the arguments to be communicated to them and, most important, the visual images that are likely to appeal to them. (Do most wear bifocals? If so, you'll have to forswear the fancy new type faces you're partial to.)

Then brainstorm, free-associate, with your co-author(s), with your spouse, with yourself. (Solitary brainstorming sessions in the shower, over a meal, on the way to/from work can be very productive.) Your objectives: (1) an idea that expresses your argument to your target audience, and (2) visual and verbal expressions of it.

Time out for a reminder: As I mentioned at the top of chapter 10, in real life (as distinct from this book), authors usually think about words and pictures simultaneously. Even if you're creating a brochure by yourself, you're thinking pictures as well as words as you free-associate, seeing covers in your mind's eye.

Of course, if you have a partner, you're brainstorming together.

You're both thinking visually and verbally until, Eureka!, you hit upon an idea that does the job. That is, *it dramatizes your argument to your target audience in a way that promises to achieve your objective within your budget and time frame.*

This idea may be visual. It may be verbal. You may call it a "strategy," "theme" or "position." Regardless, it is the heart of your communication. Once you've come up with it, you're on your way. You've provided a platform for *both* writer and art director.

Exhibit A

To illustrate the process, let's revisit how I imagine *The Economist* editorial/cover story I referenced in chapter nine might have come to be:

- **Step One.** A group of editors, writers and art directors brainstorms about how to dramatize the argument about U.S. foreign policy leadership in a way *The Economist* readers (the target audience) will find compelling.

- **Step Two.** The ideas fly thick and fast. "How about this?" "What do you think of this?" Then one of the participants says, "Stealth." And everybody else says, "That's it."

  Now, who said "Stealth"? Was it the magazine's art director, the writer who will write the piece, another editor, the janitor?

  It doesn't matter. As I mentioned earlier, ideas rarely have single parents. The best emerge from groups whose members imagine together with the most spontaneity and the least inhibition.

- **Step Three.** Once the "Stealth" idea is born and endorsed by all interested parties, at least provisionally, the writer uses it to frame the written piece:

  "The Stealth is technically amazing, powerfully effective — and also bizarrely shaped and difficult to trace. Is it not, in fact, rather like America's foreign policy?"

  The art director uses it to represent the piece visually, beginning by searching for a visual representation of the Stealth bomber that will grab the target audience (particularly that portion of it that buys *The Economist* at newsstands).

  The options are numerous (photograph, illustration, blueprint, Stealth on the ground, in the air, in combat, et. al.), and so are the restrictions: space, color, time, cost, availability.

In this instance, the art director chose a beauty shot of the Stealth in flight, seen from above against a vibrant blue sky, then positioned the words "Leadership by Stealth" immediately behind it.

A grabber.

The authors' path, then, begins with situation and cornerstones, leads to a transcendent idea (the heart), and ends with its simultaneous visual/verbal expression.

To repeat myself, the idea is key. It's hard to create a great communication without a great underlying idea. Here are several examples:

- Michelin's baby (argument: reliability; target audience: parents).
- Range Rover's play on Britishers' tendency to understate (e.g., an ad that shows the car with a party balloon tied to its front bumper headlined, "When was the last time the British were this excited about anything?").
- Absolut vodka's visual puns-in-a-bottle.
- The Marlboro man.
- Joe Camel.
- Allstate's "good hands."
- General Electric's "We bring good things to life."
- Archer Daniels Midland's "Supermarket to the world."
- Miller Lite's "Great taste. Less filling."
- Budweiser's "This Bud's for you."
- Coca-Cola's "Always Coca-Cola."
- Chevrolet's "Heartbeat of America" and "Like a rock."

And from the world of politics:

- FDR's "New Deal."
- JFK's "New Frontier."
- LBJ's "Great Society."
- George Wallace's 1968 classic "Send them a message" (argument: "Throw the rascals out"; target audience: disaffected voters).

The art of design

Once you've created a visual expression of your idea (which ties inextricably to your verbal expression of it), the next step is to design a "layout" for your communication(s). A layout is simply the various elements of your presentation positioned relative to one another.

Typically, the elements are the visualization, the lead, the body (or text), the signature and, in electronic communications, the sounds.

Good design catches your target audience's eye (and/or ear) and leads it smoothly through your argument to your bid for action and signature. It's both wonderfully dramatic and exquisitely simple; it flows, sweeps the target audience's eye from point to point, scene to scene, page to page.

It's also understated

That is, your target audience should never be aware that they're being swept from point to point, scene to scene, page to page.

Think about movies you've especially liked. Were you conscious of their design? I'll bet not. All of the artistry — performance, cinematography, scripting, staging, editing — served the story. Nothing was gratuitous. Form followed — and aided — function. Style supported — and enhanced — content.

When you're designing your communications, this is your goal.

Timeless vs. timely design

I was 15 when it happened. I fell in love. There had been others before, but this one was different.

The object of my affection was a 1946 Ford convertible. It had been chopped, channeled, sectioned, de-chromed, coated with red lacquer, and it was beguiling, dazzling, mesmerizing, choose your adjective. I got goosebumps whenever I saw it. And I saw it often. Its owner was a neighbor.

Four decades and change later, I can still see this beauty in my mind's eye, and it still looks worthy of my lust. Why? What was it about this car that so captivated me? Timeless design.

Its designer had a marvelous sense of proportion. His alterations were simultaneously subtle and striking — "radically conservative." When you saw the car for the first time, it looked familiar somehow, but different enough so that you had to look again, even if you weren't interested in cars. And when you did, what you saw wasn't familiar at all. It was unique.

Years later, I discovered that the person responsible for this masterpiece had parlayed his talent into a successful career as an automobile designer and professor of design at one of the nation's premier schools. Not exactly a surprise. He showed his genius early. And clearly.

I can recall other examples of timeless design (the Concorde, Chris Craft's "barrelback" runabout), and my hunch is, you can too. There's the equivalent of a chopped, channeled and sectioned '46 Ford in your past as well, right? Don't lose sight of it.

Today, the relevant questions are: What makes these designs timeless? And can we use whatever that is to make our communications more effective?

Or, what can we learn from the designs of the '46 Fords in our past that'll add horsepower to our communications today?

Let's start by distinguishing between "timely" and "timeless" design. The former aims to capitalize on whims of the moment. The latter is oblivious to them. Sadly, the world of communications is largely a world of timely design.

Designers typically pay close attention to what their peers in film, television, fashion and fine arts are up to, and when they see something that catches their fancy, they pile on. The titles from early James Bond films are a good example. Their snappy style quickly became the "in" thing in TV spots.

For many designers, filmmakers such as Stanley Kubrick, Ridley Scott and Sidney Lumet are idols, well worth "learning from" or, less charitably, imitating. Even in print communications. More than one designer has sought to give a "Blade Runner" cast to a capabilities brochure.

Another example of timely design: headlines that use different type faces and sizes. Have you noticed how this idea has caught on? No matter that these headlines force readers to become cryptographers.

Diagrammatic designs are also "hot" (or "cool") at the moment. Island visuals connected by dotted lines, to look "scientific," like a medial or engineering drawing or blueprint. Most look to me like a map of the Indonesian Archipelago.

The look is the substance

Much of today's timely design shares the presumption that people don't, or won't, read. Hence, to be "reader friendly" is to minimize word count and size. Legibility? Irrelevant. A paragraph of text is a design element, a building block to be positioned in a way that enhances the "look" of the communication — as opposed to its content.

What might appear to be an exception to this presumption — text whose "important" words are highlighted — is in fact an elaboration of it. The thinking goes that, because people don't read, one must splash a glob of yellow over a word to call attention to it, and no words longer than six letters, please (or "pls").

It ain't all bad

There are few absolutes in life, and eschewing timely design isn't one of them. It has its place. The issue is appropriateness. If your communication is a "telegram" to people who think MTV is "way cool," you might well want to steal a page from Quentin Tarantino's playbook. Just don't make it too hard for your audience to decipher, and don't expect to be showing it off five years from now.

This gets us to another "dark side" of timely design: It can thwart, or at least interfere with, the exchange of information. Sometimes designers get so caught up in expressing themselves, showcasing their talents, that they forget that their masterpiece is an object of communication, not an *objet d'art*.

Our job is to remind them. Gently, of course. Remind them that their mission isn't to chip away at a marble block till they expose the "David" within; it's to make the block itself irresistibly fascinating to a given group of folks. The best designers are exceptionally good at packaging information in ways that make it clear, comprehensible, attractive, interesting and easy to consume quickly. They are marvelous tailors.

First principles

This is especially true for those who practice design of the timeless sort. My precocious neighbor of yore didn't create his 1946 Ford; he simply made the package more attractive — to some people. (At the same time I was lusting after the car, others were no doubt disparaging it. "Lord, Emma, look what that crazy whippersnapper has gone and done to a perfectly good Ford.")

What's more, the young whippersnapper did this by paying attention to "first principles." It wasn't a hit movie or a trendy fashion design that inspired him. He was guided by more enduring lights: shape, scale, proportion, flow, balance, simplicity, humanity, authenticity (that is, if you have a sow's ear, make it a stunningly beautiful sow's ear).

These principles apply to communications design, too. Adhering to them, or at least considering them, likely will yield work you'll be proud of five or 10 years from now. More important, it's likely to yield work that will communicate powerfully and persuasively today.

How to judge

Art critic Leslie Fiedler once suggested that the best way to measure the quality of a work of art was to ask, "How many people has it appealed to for how long?" This strikes me as a useful way to evaluate communications designs as well.

Try it. Next time you review a design, ask yourself, "How many people in our target audience is this design likely to appeal to for how long?" Then give it a thumbs up or down based on your answer.

Be sure to listen to your gut, though. The relevant question is how do you feel about the design, not what you think of it. And the feeling that comes over you the instant you first see it is the one that counts. It's like multiple-choice questions. The more you think about them, the more likely you are to muff them.

Your first impression is, of course, the best approximation of how your target audience is apt to react. After all, for them the first impression may be the only impression. They don't study the communications that deluge them…just as you don't spend much time scrutinizing those that flood your life.

Even though producing them may be a big part of your life.

For the criteria-minded

If you're the sort who prefers a more analytical approach, I suggest that you use the first principles above as criteria. That is:

- How appealing is its shape (are its shapes) to your target audience?
- How well does the scale fit the tale?
- To what degree are the elements in balance or proportion? (Conversely, to what extent do some seem swollen, others shrunken?)
- How simple is it? (Or, to use a word that's popular among car buffs, how "clean" is it? Mark it down for irrelevant filigree.)
- How smoothly and unerringly will it lead your target audience's eyes through your argument?

    Good design lays out a clear, well-marked path from the initial point of contact (optical center) through the argument to the signature.

- How much warmth, honesty and humanity does it project?
- Does it pretend to be something it's not? (For example, a trust department brochure whose pages are laid out asymmetrically, given that asymmetry communicates verve and flare.)
- How well will it wear? (In the event your target audiences do see it repeatedly, how quickly will they tire of it? How quickly will your CEO tire of it?)
- How pleasing to the eye is it?

Score your answers on a 1-10 scale (grotesque to magnificent). See how close the total is to 90, and you'll have a good indication of the effectiveness of your design. If they don't add up to at least 80, you don't have a grabber. Return to your drawing board.

Willie who?

Among my memorabilia is a 1971 *Saturday Review* magazine cover that features one of the most compelling photographs I have ever seen. As you look at Willie Mays in midswing, you feel his extraordinary power, lightning reflexes and superlative coordination. You see the single-minded focus of his eyes. And you marvel at the grace of the man.

Unless you're my wife. For her, it's just another picture of just another baseball player.

I offer this tale as another reminder of a fact that matters enormously when you are creating visualizations for your communications: Beauty is in the eye of the beholder, a.k.a. your target audience.

Matters of proportion

In the course of writing this book, I telephoned the da Vinci who created my teenage dream car. As we reminisced about it, he talked about proportion. In his view, the key to the car's beauty was the relationships between the changes he made.

He took two inches out of the windshield, not three; three inches out of the body, not six. He removed the chrome from the hood and trunk, but kept it on the grille and bumpers. Upshot? Timeless design. Proportion matters.

In defense of filigree

Lest I come off as a crotchety minimalist ("the most beautiful object the world has ever seen is an egg"), I do believe there are occasions when hot fudge, whipped cream and a cherry make ice cream tastier. Take the Chrysler Building.

Eight hundred feet in the air, far from the eyes of the crowds below are...
gargoyles. Can you imagine how the Chrysler executives must have reacted when
the architect presented this idea? "You want to spend our hard-earned money —
money that could go to profits or plants or employees' paychecks — to put gargoyles
where no one can see them? Have you talked to your doctor about this?"

To their credit, they went along with the gag, and their successors have been, and
will continue to be, well-rewarded. Those creatures and the design they are part of
have inspired countless millions for 65 years and will for a long time to come.

How many have bought Chryslers or gone to work for Chrysler or loaned Chrysler
money as a result? Who knows? Enough, I'll bet, to have paid for those gargoyles a
thousand times over.

Moral: Don't reject filigree out of hand. It can be a wonderful touch. Do ask yourself how it fits and whether it adds to the power of the communication.

Timeless passing fancies

Isn't it a contradiction to design something so ephemeral as a sales presentation
or brochure to be timeless? Why bother? If it delivers its message a time or two,
hasn't it done its job?

Not entirely. I see three reasons to strive for timeless design. First, it can become a
framework or create a standard for your communications that can last for many years.

Second, in a world of timely design, timeless designs stand out and add "oomph"
to all your communications, even those that will be history in a week or month.

Finally, the pursuit itself is inspiring, energizing, ennobling and rewarding.
Everyone involved will walk a little taller for making the effort.

So go for it! And let your equivalent of my '46 Ford be your guiding light.

The design of the creative process

Situation + Cornerstones

---

to

Idea (a.k.a. strategy, theme, position)

---

to

Visualization
Headline
Body
Close

---

to

Layout

Chapter 12

Matters of Style

Executive Summary

Objective:

Rework your communications without wreaking havoc on their irresistibility.

Strategies:

(1) Convince prospective reworkers that communications are indivisible units, not collections of parts that can be individually altered.

That is, when you change one thing, you change the whole thing.

(2) Convince prospective reworkers that communications are stylistically fragile and "nitpicking" threatens their stylistic integrity.

That is, there's no such thing as a "little change."

(3) Convince prospective reworkers that style matters. Communications that have it are more likely to get heard by more members of their target audiences.

(4) Acknowledge to prospective reworkers that style is subjective and so the question is not, "Is it right?" but rather, "Is it right for us?"

That is, is it consistent with the way your organization comports itself?

(5) Remind prospective reworkers that the more they analyze your communications, the greater the distance they put between them and your target audiences.

First reactions are usually the best reactions. Trust them.

(6) When changes must be made, insist that the authors make them. Maintain a clear division of labor between managers and editors, on the one hand, and authors, on the other.

Managers and editors criticize. Authors conceive. (The yin and yang of the creative process.)

  • Authors will help their cause if they recognize that managers and editors are human…and so aren't always able to express their criticisms clearly. It pays to listen "between the lines."

- Managers and editors will help their cause if they recognize that authors' angry first reactions to their criticisms are teapot tempests that can be safely ignored. A 24-hour "cooling-off period" is usually all it takes.

(7) Don't submit your communications to protracted deliberations. Like doughnuts and coffee, they're best when fresh. So decide, implement and get on to the next assignment.

"Golly, maybe we should have left it the way it was."

Imagine. You're a fly on the wall of a meeting room in Maranello, Italy. The year is 1983, and you're eavesdropping on a conversation between two legends, Enzo Ferrari, the man who founded and oversees the car company, and Pinin Farina, founding head of the firm that designs most of Ferrari's cars. Here's what you hear:

Ferrari: Pinin, I think the design you've come up with for our new Testarossa is excellent.

Farina: Thank you, Enzo.

Ferrari: But I do have a few concerns, little things.

Farina: What are they, Enzo?

Ferrari: I think the rearview mirrors stick out too far, and the taillights aren't round enough. Also, the bumper guards ought to be chrome-plated, and, oh yes, the Ferrari emblem on the hood needs to be much bigger.

Farina: But, Enzo, these little things are really big things. If I were to make these changes, the feeling of the car would change. It wouldn't be the same car. I'm sorry, Enzo, but I can't make them. I have to be true to the integrity of the design.

We're all nitpickers

Hard to imagine, isn't it? One grand master nitpicking another's styling. A little like painting a mustache on the Mona Lisa. And yet, we who are involved in communications do it often.

We do it for numerous reasons. Some of us don't really believe the style or artistry of an ad or a brochure matters all that much. Does it make the points we want it to make? Is it legible? Are the logo and phone number big and bold? These are the things that count.

We also tend to underestimate the impact of nitpicking on our communications' effectiveness. We tell ourselves, like Enzo Ferrari never did, that our nitpicks are "little things" that won't make much difference. Even the term "nitpicking" serves to reinforce this delusion.

What's more, there are certain practicalities that can't be ignored. What the lawyers think, for example, and the techies, and the CEO. And the customers we heard from in our focus groups.

So we compromise. Move this picture, change that paragraph, add a "virtually" here and an "exciting" there, make the logo bigger, "pump up" the headline…all without paying much attention to the communication's style. It still looks OK, nice and colorful. And the sales folks love it. Hell, it'll do the job.

Maybe. Maybe not. What's almost certain is that it will have lost its artistry — assuming it had artistry to begin with. And artistry is power. Art moves people. And art, by definition, has what I call "integrity of style."

The editor's path

What if your position requires you to judge the creations of others? In this case, your task is to initiate, guide and critique in ways that lead to bigger, better, bolder ideas. This usually means staying aloof from the brainstorming process — a difficult thing to do.

You call your authors together, discuss the assignment, agree on a schedule, review situation and cornerstones, toss out an idea or two to prime the pump, and withdraw.

From then on, your role is to review and comment insightfully on their brainstormings at regular, predetermined intervals. Again, you may toss out an idea or two to galvanize the process — with no pride of authorship.

There are two keys to successful editing: (1) trust your initial reactions — that's when your mindset is most akin to your target audience's (your "first blush" will be their only blush). (2) Be absolutely candid and honest with your authors — if you feel "yuck," say "yuck."

Raising goosebumps

Think about the times you've experienced integrity of style. It may have been when a Testarossa cruised past, or when you went to the ballet and saw a classic *pas de deux*. Or the moment may have been more prosaic. A Penn Warren poem, perhaps, or a "Far Side" cartoon, or the time you sat in an Eames chair.

No matter. Do you recall how you felt? My hunch is, one of those wows that we talked about in chapter nine may have escaped your lips, or the skin on the back of your neck came alive, or a smile flashed across your face, or you felt goosebumps on your arms. It was exciting.

Communications that have integrity of style can trigger the same reactions, which makes them enormously persuasive. They are the bell ringers — the speeches, ads, brochures, videos, slide shows, et. al. that pay for themselves (and their lesser brethren) many times over. They are also what serious writers, art directors and designers set out to create every time they put pen to paper or fingers to keyboards.

They fall short most of the time, of course, just as we all do. But they never stop trying — it's their Holy Grail — and they realize that what will get them there is integrity of style. So when they feel they've created something that has it, something that will cause their target audiences to whisper "Wow!" to themselves, they resist others' well-meaning attempts to amend or "improve" their work. "Change isn't always for the better," they argue.

"I've been mugged!"

A writer friend once created a newspaper ad he was especially proud of. His client responded favorably, asked for but a single word change. Unfortunately, the word, which appeared in the headline, was the ad's linchpin, and its loss did major damage to the integrity of the ad's style.

My friend's reaction to the client's dictate: "I've been mugged!" The offending word: "gall," as in "has the gall to…" Its replacement: "nerve." Can you feel the difference between "gall" and "nerve"? That's integrity of style.

Now, obviously, there are times when words and pictures must be changed. Not all nitpicking is irrelevant. The challenge is to make changes without compromising your communications' integrity of style. How to do this? I have a suggestion.

A modest proposal

For starters, let's agree on two things: First, we're not talking about content, only style; *how* something gets expressed, not *what* gets expressed. Content is a cornerstone, a given.

Second, a point I belabored in each of the last three chapters: An ad, brochure, speech or slide show is stylistically indivisible, a singular unit, no more a collection of separable parts than a poem or symphony is, or a Testarossa, or a person. Imagine getting a crew cut and thinking you've only changed the way the top of your head looks.

When we change a word, picture or typeface, we change the overall appearance of the communication, by definition. So we ought to at least be sensitive to the effect of our changes on its integrity of style.

Better yet — and here's my proposal — if we didn't create the communication, we should not rework it. Let its authors rework it. We should simply explain our stylistic concerns to the authors and let them figure out how to resolve these concerns. They're much more likely to preserve their creation's artistic integrity than we are.

For the record, when I write "authors," I include writer, art director and designer, as well as producer, director, cinematographer and editor in the case of video.

Style is where you find it

Hurrying through the bowels of Chicago's O'Hare Airport one day en route to the subway station, I came upon a poster that stopped me in my tracks. A large, full-color photograph showed a shirtless rock climber halfway up a sheer cliff. One arm and one leg are flying free as he searches for his next toe- and hand-holds. The picture is captioned, "Can you believe this maniac? No sunscreen." The copy reminds us that skin cancer will afflict one in five of us. The poster's sponsors: the American Academy of Dermatology and the U.S. Public Health Service. An inspired communication, stylistically perfect, conceptually brilliant.

A healthy division

Leaving "rewrites" to the writers creates a healthy division of labor — authors create, editors and managers critique — the benefits of which are three:

- It increases the likelihood that your communications will have integrity of style.
- It forces authors to take responsibility for their work.
- It eliminates (I hope) the possibility of euphemisms.

On the second point, when writers, art directors and designers operate under the assumption that their task is simply to provide "first drafts" for managers to amend, they can convince themselves that they're not really responsible for the effectiveness of the communication in its finished form.

On the other hand, if they know from the get-go that the finished work will be their baby and that their performance will be measured by its performance, chances are, they'll make a much better baby.

Regarding euphemisms, I know I've assailed them already, but they're had to get rid of, so I want to take another swipe. *They are the worst.* They destroy stylistic integrity as surely as Raid kills ants, because they signal target audiences that the communication's sponsor isn't prepared to talk straight.

Trouble is, people who focus on content as well as style may not be as alert to euphemisms as they should be. They can sneak past a manager, but they will never get by an author.

Almost right Bach

I like Bach, but give me Bach by three good orchestras, and I won't be able to hear stylistic differences that are like fingernails on a blackboard to musicians. ("The violins are flat.")

But show me three solutions to the same assignment by three good writer/art director/designer teams, and I'll be able to spot the subtlest of stylistic imperfections. That's because I've spent my life making and judging communications.

So it seems unfair to ask people whose relationship approximates mine to orchestral interpretations of Bach to see and fix stylistic flaws that make communications almost right.

Let authors create and editors and managers critique, and your communications will have greater integrity of style and more ear-opening power.

Remember, when it comes to communications, "almost right" is wrong.

A word to managers and editors

The cover art was stunning. The artist had painted an exquisite *trompe l'oeil*. Both the tree and the woodpecker in it were perfect. Too perfect. People who saw it were put off by the burl on the tree's trunk.

When we asked the artist to change it, he was horrified, then irate. He brought us the photographs he'd used to help him, showed us how accurately he'd represented the burl. We tried to explain that what mattered in this instance was perception, not reality. But he wasn't listening. He was fuming. He grabbed his masterpiece and stormed out of our meeting.

Forty-eight hours later, he and his masterpiece were back, minus the burl. In its place, plain old bark. Lovely bark. The booklet was well-received, especially its cover, even by the company's environmental critics.

Moral: When you ask one of your communication's authors to make stylistic changes, get ready for an angry reaction and take comfort in the knowledge that it will be short-lived. A day's cooling off is usually all it takes.

I can say this with some confidence because, as my colleagues will attest, I've experienced those angry reactions many, many times — inside myself. And they're impossible to sustain for very long.

I'll let you in on a secret. Most authors don't fly off the handle because they're high-strung, temperamental prima donnas; they get angry because *they don't know how to fix the burl*. Their anger hides their fear.

When a manager tells me something I created has to be changed, my first reaction is interior panic. Change to what? I don't know! And I have to figure it out! So what do I do? I yell out a four-letter word that starts with "s" and ends with "t" and carries two conflicting inferences: "I feel angry" and "I feel that I'm in trouble."

Half an hour later, the brain lock I experienced when I first got the bad news has disappeared. I've talked about the problem with my art director partner, and I've started to free-associate. At this point, I know I'll come up with a solution, probably within a day or two. And guess what? I'm not angry anymore. Or scared.

By the way, there are two other possible explanations for author tantrums you should be aware of (if you're not already):

- "If you don't like every single thing about my creation, it must not be any good, and so I must not be any good, which means I'm about to lose my livelihood, and I don't have any other. I'm doomed!"
- "You've added to my workload just when I was planning to take the afternoon off."

A word to the authors

If you're a writer, art director or designer with the scars to prove it, I have a one-word prescription that I guarantee will make your life easier and your work better: listen.

Listen with care, attention and compassion to your editors' and managers' concerns. Listen with the understanding that they're human and so may not be able to articulate their concerns clearly.

I had a client once who drove me nuts with his rewrites of my copy. One day, my frustration boiled over, and I went to see him, aiming to have a showdown. "If you want me to write your copy, keep your mitts off!" I was prepared to say. But I didn't have to. When I expressed my frustration, he apologized profusely, saying he didn't mean to propose alternative words but rather to question mine.

When we got this straight, we were able to work through his concerns quickly and painlessly. Most of the time, when I explained why I chose the words I did, his concerns evaporated. When they didn't, I'd come up with alternatives that eased his worries without compromising the integrity of style I was worried about.

It's exceedingly rare that there's only one right word, picture or layout, and in those instances ("gall," for example), an honest explanation will almost always carry the day. As long as you've listened first.

The infernal subjectivity of it all

As you know (and as I mentioned in chapter nine), when it comes to style, one person's "Wow!" is another's "Yuck!" We all have our particular likes and dislikes, including the people in your target audience. The question is how to reconcile them without diminishing the effectiveness of your communication.

I'll tackle this question in detail in chapter 17. For the moment, let me offer these suggestions:

- When you and your colleagues get together to discuss/debate matters of style, start by reminding yourselves that you're dealing with subjective issues and that, no matter how you resolve them, you'll leave some in your target audience dissatisfied...because your target audience members don't see eye to eye on style issues either.

- This being the case, the important questions become, "What are most of them most likely to cotton to?" And, "Is it right for us?" That is, "Does it square with the way our organization behaves?"

  The information you gathered about your target audience when you were building your initiative's cornerstones should help you address both of these questions.

- One way to minimize style headaches is to identify authors whose style is consistent with your organization's and stick with them. The more they work with you, the more attuned they become to your outfit's character and personality, the fewer your headaches. Remember, the grass is rarely greener.

Style doesn't age well

Has this ever happened to you? Peerless Communications presents a full-color mock-up of a 24-page capabilities brochure to Acme International's six-person executive committee. All six are very complimentary ("great job," "looks terrific," "really creative," "how soon can we have it?"), especially Acme's communications VP.

After the meeting, he takes the mock-up back to his office and puts it on his coffee table. For the next week or so, everyone who comes into his office — including his five fellow excom members, eight media reps, each of his 12 direct reports and his two teenaged kids — takes note of the mock-up, leafs through it and makes an editorial comment or two ("nice picture, why is it so green?" and "sure wish the charts were bigger").

Two weeks later, at the next excom meeting, when the capabilities brochure project comes up for discussion, the communications VP tells his cohorts he's not happy with it and it needs a lot of work...and they all agree ("maybe we ought to give Matchless Communications a shot at the project").

As you know if this sort of thing has happened to you, it's a rare piece of communication that can withstand repeated second-guessing from interested parties who probably don't know the cornerstones it was built on...and a rare communications executive who can remain impervious to repeated second guesses.

That's because communications typically aren't created to be scrutinized, analyzed and dissected like a laboratory animal. They're created to be experienced, enjoyed and discarded.

Most communications are like coffee, bread and brownies: best when fresh.

Chapter 13

Teaming Up

Executive Summary

Objective:

Assemble a team of communications people that creates irresistible communications, quickly, consistently and painlessly.

Strategies:

(1) Base your candidate selection in part on your judgment of their inclination and ability to work intimately with other communications professionals.

(2) Create a physical environment that's conducive to teamwork — comfortable chairs, plenty of whiteboards (with colored markers), tackable walls (with tacks), an oval table, good lighting and acoustics, windows to the outside (very important), easy access to technology, food and beverages.

(3) Schedule a series of at least four meetings at times when everyone can participate. Make sure everyone understands that she/he is an important player in an important effort.

(4) Minimize constraints, particularly time constraints. Make it clear that get-togethers are informal, open-ended and free-form, Urge your mates to dress for comfort and pocket their watches.

(5) Reminisce about successful and unsuccessful teams. Point out that a collection of all-stars is rarely an all-star team, that working together works wonders. Cite examples from your personal experience.

(6) Define the assignment precisely. Review situation, cornerstones and team objective (amazing strategies and tactics, a.k.a. "great ideas").

(7) Get personal. Invite team members to talk with one another about hometowns, families, hobbies, heroes, pets, pet peeves, books, movies, etc. Make sure they discover their shared interests.

(8) Confront stereotypes. Imaginative people are often shy, insecure and, hence, reluctant to stop playing their professional "roles" and simply be themselves.

One way to deal with this reluctance is to have fun with it and poke fun at it. The idea is to *be* together.

(9) Lead by example. Start free-associating yourself, then invite others to join you "when they feel like it."

(10) Encourage trespassing. Urge researchers to invent copy lines and writers to suggest media vehicles, but make it clear that, come judgment day, you'll look to writers for copy, media mavens for media vehicles, etc., so there's no competition; everyone's the master of his/her universe.

(11) Point out that "big ideas" rarely have single parents. They tend to take shape through a succession of free associations over time and, when they come, they belong to the team.

(12) Remind your mates that the whole will be greater than the sum of its parts; that is, "Together, we'll create a more ambitious, inspired initiative than any one or two of us could dream up on our own."

(13) Remind them, too, that what matters is the initiative as a whole, not its component parts. In this case, Vince Lombardi was right: Winning is the only thing. There's no glory — or money — for individuals who star in a losing effort.

(14) Include the people who pay the bills. Clients, be they from other departments or other organizations, have much to offer…once they and their new teammates get comfortable *being* together.

(15) Be candid to signal your mates that it's important for them to be candid, too. It's hard to free-associate when everyone's being diplomatic, making "nice-nice."

(16) Be patient.

"Now listen up, men!"

CAVEAT: *Getting Heard* is not a team-building book. Others know far more about team-building than I, and they've put what they know into books you can buy through the catalog put out by the publisher of this book or at your favorite bookstore.

I have learned some things about assembling and managing teams of communications people, though, having done so with some success (and more than a few failures) for quite some time. I'll share them with you in this chapter. I hope you find them useful.

Walter was among the most able business people I've ever worked with. He had been retained to bail out one of my clients, a cruise line that was about to go down for the third time. His contract called for him to spend four days a week at this task — which left him three days and seven nights a week to oversee a successful regional airline and advise the U.S. Travel Service.

Unfortunately for most of those who worked for him, he was also the most intimidating person I've ever worked with. No matter that he was barely 5 feet 6 inches tall; that he spoke seldom, quietly and courteously; that he listened attentively, never lost his temper and laughed easily. He scared the wits out of his subordinates — literally.

When I'd present my work, Walter would typically say nothing. Long minutes would pass. Silence (one of his favorite tools). In time, he'd turn to one of his vice presidents. "Well, what do you think?" he'd say, whereupon the poor fellow would try frantically and unsuccessfully to discern what his boss wanted to hear, finally mumbling some noncommittal thing like, "Very interesting."

From Walter I learned a great deal — his rescue operation was brilliant — including how not to lead a team.

And then there was Don.

"Round up the usual suspects, Bobbe"

With these words, Don would instruct his secretary to organize a meeting of his communications team, as rambunctious a collection of egos as ever graced a conference room.

But wonderful things happened when this gang got together. We created spectacularly effective work, and we had a grand and uproarious time doing it. We laughed, cheered, jeered, argued, raged, yelled, cajoled and wheedled. The battle between solicitousness and truth-telling was no contest. What was felt got said. We were a team. We worked together for nine years with nary a defection, until our captain retired.

They were the happiest, most stimulating years of my professional life…so far.

Three keys to success

There were three reasons for this happy confederation. First, we had a great leader. He made each of us feel valuable, important and secure. He encouraged us to speak our minds and hearts, then listened attentively and responded constructively when we did. He made it clear that there was no such thing as a stupid idea, question or comment. Everything was useful for what it might lead to.

When there were disagreements, he refereed disinterestedly, but he was not at all disinterested himself. He touted his many self-described "great ideas" with vociferous enthusiasm, though he never took either his ideas or himself especially seriously.

Laughter, the great tonic

Which gets us to the second reason why our collaboration was so successful. We took our work seriously, but not ourselves. Humor was our secret weapon, wit an invisible ally. We poked fun at ourselves and at one another, and we made it a point to inject jokes, cartoons, drawings and stories into our meetings to sustain their tempo.

During a particularly noisy and largely irrelevant argument, one team member stood up and with great fanfare announced, "I think I have entered a parallel universe."

Everyone's a master

Reason number three was that everyone explicitly acknowledged everyone else's bailiwick and expertise. Yes, there was trespassing, plenty of it, mostly in the form of uninvited suggestions — no shrinking violets in this group. But, at the end of the debate, our captain tilted to the person responsible for the subject of the debate. That is, when we argued about the questions on a survey questionnaire, the views of our research guru counted most.

This made for a wonderfully supportive environment. Your teammates understood that you were the master of your universe. You had the power, so you didn't have to struggle for it. You could relax, think out loud, be spontaneous. The mood was collegial. No one postured or took potshots. We enjoyed one another and our times together.

The whole was greater

In sum, we functioned like a well-coached basketball or soccer team. We knew our positions and played them well, we knew that teamwork was essential to our success and we all recognized that, together, we could create things that were bigger and better than any of us could create individually. There was no ball hogging.

Moral: As the "usual suspects" demonstrated, teamwork can indeed work wonders when there is effective leadership, a congenial climate and clear delineations of roles, responsibilities and authority.

The biggest obstacle

When I was a creative director in search of a "big idea," I used to do something heretical: I'd invite media planners, researchers and account managers to my creative groups' brainstorming sessions.

Putting these people around the same table was akin to inviting members of the ACLU, the IRA, the KKK, the Christian Coalition and the Flat Earth Society to lunch. Everyone was wary, lest she or he say something "dumb" or "foolish."

But as the participants came to realize that there was no such thing as "dumb" or "foolish," they began to loosen up, and the sparks began to fly.

These were imaginative people, and they inevitably came up with amazing stuff once they stopped performing and started thinking; that is, once they stopped being scared and started free-associating, once they were able to say to themselves, "Hey, I can do this, and it's fun!"

What got in their way, and what I had to deal with as their captain, were the stereotypes they held of their colleagues and themselves. Writers and art directors had to be clever. Media planners and researchers had to be analytical. Account managers had to be glib, managerial, diplomatic.

I had to persuade them to stop playing these roles before I could get them to "work wonders" as a team. If you face this sort of challenge, you may be interested in the techniques I used.

Transcending fear

You've collected your "usual suspects," your communications team. They're all sitting around a conference table, bantering from behind their masks. How do you get them to put these masks aside?

For me, *Step One* was to create a physical environment that was conducive to teamwork — comfortable chairs, plenty of whiteboards (with red, blue, black and green markers), tackable walls (with tacks), an oval table, good lighting and acoustics, windows to the outside (very important), easy access to technology, food and beverages.

Step Two was to set an objective for the brainstorming sessions and to schedule a series of at least four of them at times when everyone could participate. I wanted the team to see how much importance I attached to the process and their participation in it. I wanted them to say to themselves, "This is a big deal and I'm a big part of it."

Step Three was to minimize time pressures. "Our meetings will be informal, freeform and open-ended," I'd say. "There's no hurry. Take off your watches, your ties and, if it makes you more comfortable, your shoes. We'll spend as much time as it takes. If you feel like telling a story, standing on your head or taking a walk, feel free." I also wanted team members to relax.

(To get people to relax in meetings, the head of a Los Angeles ad agency sometimes gets up from her chair, stretches a bit, then sits down on the floor.)

Step Four was to reminisce about successful and unsuccessful teams. "A collection of all-stars does not an all-star team make," I'd say, and I'd point to the 1948 Boston Red Sox baseball team, a collection of great players that lost the pennant to a supposedly lesser Cleveland nine. Conversely, Boston's basketball team, the Celtics, dominated their sport for a decade with a dozen good players in perfect sync.

Step Five was to define the assignment precisely, to make sure everyone understood the ground rules (cornerstones) and our goal (amazing communications strategies and tactics, a.k.a. "big ideas").

Step Six was an invitation of sorts. I asked team members to talk to their mates about their hometowns, families, hobbies, avocations, heroes, pets, pet peeves, favorite books and movies. People typically show only their work faces on the job, and I wanted my team to get a fuller sense of one another. It's easier to get comfortable with someone when you both discover that you share a passion for mountain biking.

Step Seven was to confront the stereotypes, to have fun with them and poke fun at them. I pointed out how art directors and copywriters are supposed to be quickwitted, sharp-tongued and flamboyant when in fact many of them, including me, are shy, introspective, moody and given to fits of masochism.

I "became" a media planner and a researcher from central casting, lowering my voice, speaking monotonously, ticking off facts and figures upon facts and figures; then, suddenly, I switched gears, put on my dancing shoes and metamorphosized into Willie Loman-cum-Uriah Heap. *Voila!* I was the stereotypical shameless account manager.

The effect of these performances was to diminish the inhibiting power of the stereotypes, to get people to question them. My performances, however, as animated as they were, did not persuade my mates to put aside their masks. They simply got them to consider the possibility.

It took *Step Eight* to convince my team that they could safely shed their masks, be themselves and think out loud. *Step Eight* consisted of me doing it as opposed to talking about it. I'd state the arguments, characterize the target audience and say whatever came into my mind — two or three or five things, very quickly. Then I'd ask a teammate what popped into her mind when I said what I'd said. Pretty soon, we were off and running, fearlessly, on our way to a "big idea" or two.

Other reassurances

Encourage trespassing. Tease copy lines out of your media planner and visualizations out of your researcher. Get your art director and copywriter to make media selections. Then take these ideas to the team members whose bailiwick they belong in and invite reactions. Pretty soon your team will be batting their ideas back and forth without your leadership, and the energy level in the room will take a quantum leap. Teamwork in action.

Incidentally, inside every researcher, account manager and media maven lurk a poet and a Picasso trying to break free. And I've yet to meet a writer or art director who didn't know the perfect media vehicle to carry his or her work.

Encourage candor. By being candid, your teammates will quickly (and gratefully) get the idea that it's important to say what they think and feel — without self-censorship. It's hard to free-associate when you're being diplomatic, making "nice-nice."

Point out that big ideas rarely have single parents. As I've mentioned previously, they tend to take shape through a succession of free associations — over time. (Hence, the value of a series of scheduled meetings to air what I call "morning afterthinking.") One person may verbalize the idea, but everyone who participates is a co-author. And it belongs to the team.

Ask, *"Who benefits?"* We all tend to be prisoners of our perspectives and to lose sight of the fact that it's only the initiative as a whole that matters, not its components. So it's useful to remind your team from time to time that everyone shares a common interest: a "world's greatest" initiative. Only then will anyone benefit.

If Vince Lombardi had been talking about communications when he said "Winning is the only thing," I'd have agreed with him. In our game, there's no glory for individuals who star in a losing effort.

Feeling cocky? Try this

Your team is working wonders. Its members have jettisoned their masks and fears and have become a well-oiled brainstorming machine. It's time to up the ante, make the move that, if you handle it right, will turn your league leaders into world champs. It's time to invite a few people from your client's organization to join your team.

If you work for a consulting firm, your client is, of course, the organization that's paying your invoices. If you work in the communications or marketing department of a company, your client may be another department, a business unit or the CEO. Regardless, it's almost always the case that clients are smart people who have valuable insights to contribute — and who are just as capable of inspired brainstorming as you and your teammates are.

The rub is, like Walter, they tend to shut everybody down. "Oh, we have to be careful, have to watch what we say and how we act. There are clients in the house." In other words, when clients arrive, the masks go back on. Until and unless you seize the moment, and do what you have to do to get those masks removed again.

And, by the way, you'll have a couple more to deal with this time around. Clients wear masks, too.

It's worth it, though. When you have a client or two on your communications team, it will work wonders. Guaranteed.

Untying a giant's tongue, an exercise in patience

A decade earlier, the company's long-time CEO had made an off-hand remark that quickly made it onto the company grapevine and into its culture. "The spouting whale gets harpooned," he said.

What he meant was "Don't spout off; make sure you have something substantial to say before you open your mouth," but his employees took him to mean, "Be silent; let others communicate on your behalf."

As a result, attempts by the company's corporate and marketing communications people to put essential programs in place were half-baked and short-lived. We were retained to come up with a campaign that would overcome the company's inhibitions and enable it to communicate its corporate and product strengths to dealers, buyers, users and influencers around the world.

Gulp. We quickly decided that we needed to add firepower, so we recruited four top freelancers to join our team — two designers and two writers. The four knew one another, but had never worked together. They saw themselves, correctly, as rivals.

The ultimate challenge was to break through our client's inhibitions; the immediate challenge was to break through our own. Our early meetings were like poker games: Everyone was suffocatingly circumspect, careful not to show ideas others might put down.

Fortunately, these were smart people who recognized the stakes, warmed to the challenge and one another and eventually created brilliant, successful work — which, by the way, included a humorous ghostwritten bulletin from the CEO to all employees explaining the real intent of his famous remark.

The key word was "eventually." The process of moving from wary poker player rival to intimate collaborator couldn't be hurried. But it paid off. And it taught us all that patience is both a virtue and an essential part of teamwork.

Chapter 14

McLuhan Was Right

Executive Summary

Objective:

Choose media that fit — and enhance — the message.

Strategies:

(1) Gain a communications strategist's working knowledge of the attributes of various media vehicles.

To develop effective strategies, you need to be able to juggle information in your head about art, copy, media and your cornerstones.

(2) The world of media is pervasive and constantly changing. Hence, good communications strategists never stop paying attention to it.

(3) Take newspapers. Once they were a mass medium. Today, their readers are largely college-educated, literate, middle-aged and older, who read newspapers for background information, color and commentary. They get their news from radio and television.

Communications strategists lean to newspapers when the target audience is literate and the arguments complex.

(4) Magazines, too, have evolved. Large-circulation, general-interest magazines have given way to a plethora of special-interest publications. If more than a dozen people do it, there's a magazine about it.

For communications strategists, magazines are the medium of choice when the target audience is selective.

(5) Direct mail offers no-waste coverage of your target audience if you're able to define it precisely. It also offers a high degree of interactivity, personalization and creative flexibility.

On the other hand, it's extremely expensive and there's no guarantee your message won't travel directly from your target audience's mailbox to their garbage can, especially given the volume of mail nowadays.

(6) Radio thrives, particularly FM, although talk radio, led by Rush Limbaugh, has given AM a new lease on life. Because radio is a background medium,

messages have to reach out as well as stand out. Programming delivers some audience selectivity.

Communications strategists turn to radio when the argument is clear and straightforward, the audience selective, the budget modest and the client anxious to "get started." You can be on-air in a matter of hours.

(7) Television is in the midst of a continuing revolution. More networks, more channels, UHF, VHF, cable, pay-per-view, satellite, ads in disguise on public television stations, cable modems and Web TV so people can "watch" the Internet.

Communications strategists view television as a uniquely powerful, if expensive, media vehicle because it combines sight, sound and motion (and so is the next best thing to a salesperson in the target audience's living room), because it reaches huge audiences and because it offers tremendous creative flexibility.

Drawbacks: Audiences aren't particularly selective, and they'll zap your message if it's not instantly riveting; the landscape is cluttered with huckstering *ad nauseam*; TV ads are expensive to produce.

(8) The new medium on the block is the World Wide Web. It's growing rapidly (some say so rapidly that it's doomed to collapse), offers a wide variety of ways to use it, attracts intelligent, youthful audiences and offers great creative flexibility and interactivty.

(9) As the mainstream media's costs and noise levels climb, communications strategists pay more attention to alternatives such as:

- trade shows
- forums, seminars, symposia
- skywriting
- pamphleteering
- 3D billboards
- kiosks
- video mailings
- public broadcasting underwriting

(10) Media selection criteria revisited (from chapter two):

- *Affordability.* Make sure you know how much the media you're considering cost and that you can afford them.
- *Reach.* Make sure they cover your target audience.
- *Frequency.* Make sure you communicate to your target audience repeatedly or your messages won't register.
- *Efficiency.* Target audience/dollar, the basic way to compare media vehicles.
- *Context.* How well does the medium fit your message? Does its editorial direction complement the messages you want to deliver? If so, that's a big, but incalculable, plus.

"Hmmm. What am I missing here?"

Just as you can't solve a physics problem until you know all the variables, you can't devise effective communications strategies until you're familiar with:

(1) the nature of the arguments

(2) the nature of the target audience, including media consumption habits and preferences

(3) the communications objective

(4) the budget

(5) the time frame

(6) the most powerful ways of dramatizing the arguments

(7) the attributes of the various media

So far we've covered the first five variables in our discussions of cornerstones and the sixth in our discussions of message-making. In this chapter, we'll focus on the one that remains: media attributes.

The expanding universe

To be a communications strategist is to have to keep up with a media world that, thanks mostly to microchips, grows more ubiquitous and complicated every day. Take newspapers.

There are morning newspapers, afternoon newspapers, dailies, weeklies, monthlies. There are national, regional, metro, suburban and neighborhood newspapers; newspapers devoted to particular groups, professions, causes, activities and hobbies; free sheets, broadsheets, fax sheets, tabloids and controlled-circulation journals. There are electronic newspapers that you access via computer.

In fact, you can tailor an electronic newspaper of your very own, so you don't waste precious moments flipping through your local fish wrap in search of articles that interest you. Of course, this presumes that you know today what will interest you tomorrow, which sort of defeats the basic purpose of a newspaper, doesn't it?

It certainly points up a fundamental change in the role of newspapers. People no longer turn to them to find out what's going on — radio and TV tell them that. They look to newspapers to add dimension to what they already know. They heard the final score of the Dallas-New York game on their radios five minutes after it ended. From their newspaper, they want detail, color, commentary.

At least those who still read newspapers do. Paradoxically, as the number and kind of newspapers have grown, readership has declined. Once considered a local mass medium and supported primarily by local retailers, today's newspapers typically reach only 60 percent of the residents in their community and less than one-third of its "Generation X."

Who's kidding whom?

An ad agency surveyed 100 viewers of a TV mini-series to test their recall of the ads that ran in it. Among the survey's findings:

- 32 percent said they recalled Kodak ads and 32 percent said they remembered seeing Prudential ads
- 28 percent claimed to have seen Budweiser ads and 28 percent said they saw American Express ads
- 19 percent recalled seeing ads for Volkswagen.

This despite the fact that none of these companies advertised during the mini-series.

From *Times* to *Time*

At a time when more people read less and most people get their news primarily from television, newspapers have become what news magazines used to be. Their readers tend to be educated, literate and at least middle-aged. They also tend to read their newspapers differently than their parents did. They spend less time reading the main news sections, more time reading the sports and entertainment sections. They may scan page one, but then they start hopping, from section to section and headline to headline.

Newspapers also have become far more colorful. Even *The New York Times*, long nicknamed "The Old Gray Lady," now publishes full-color ads. Most major papers, led by the splashy *USA Today*, also feature color in their editorial.

In these last six paragraphs, I've given you the sorts of things a communications strategist typically knows about this particular media vehicle. Who "consumes" it and why, how, when and where. Additionally, he/she will know roughly how much newspaper advertising costs and how long it takes to buy space in, and produce ads for, this vehicle.

Inside knowledge

Finally, a good strategist will know something about how newspapers are created, assembled, printed and distributed. It was this sort of "inside" knowledge that enabled one strategist I know to create a two-sided one-eighth-page coupon ad. He arranged with the publisher to place the ad in the lower right corner of a right-hand page, so readers could easily see both sides and clip the ad.

Another strategist used her working knowledge of newspapers to put together a campaign whose ads called attention to each other by page number ("to learn more about…, see page 12"). Publishers were permitted to choose which days to run the ads in return for agreeing to coordinate and add page numbers to them.

Worth remembering, if you have an idea that requires something special from a media vehicle, don't hesitate to propose it. Worst case, you get turned down. Best case, your idea becomes a standard, like "island" ads in magazines (quarter-page ads positioned in the center of a page and surrounded on all sides by editorial).

From *Time* to…?

If newspapers now deliver what people used to look to news magazines for, what do news magazines now deliver? Tales from the world of entertainment, human-interest stories, personal opinions and gossip mostly.

What was considered "back of the book" stuff a generation ago (or "soft news") has become most of the book today. *Time* has become more like its sister publication, *People*, as *People* has become more like its tabloid rivals, who, by the way, are out to become more like *Time* used to be. A couple of them have even opened news bureaus in Washington, D.C. (Time will tell, pun intended, whether their aim is news or dirt.)

With the exception of the news magazines and *Reader's Digest*, the large-circulation, general-interest magazines have disappeared, replaced by network television.

Special-interest magazines have proliferated…and continue to proliferate. Magazine start-ups are near an all-time high.

You name the occupation, interest, activity, hobby or avocation, and I'll bet you there are at least two magazines devoted to it. Skateboarding, wood carving, trekking, quilting, cigar smoking, you name it, and there's a magazine for it.

Technology also has enabled magazines to carve up their circulations in many ways. News magazines, for example, not only offer advertisers regional, state and metro editions, they also offer them demographic editions (students, doctors) and ZIP code editions. This enables advertisers to customize their messages (for a price). If you subscribe to a news magazine, you may have noticed ads in it that address you by name. (Pseudo-personalization.)

Manna from heaven

All this is manna from heaven for communications strategists with very selective target audiences. It's the functional equivalent of direct mail with the magazine as envelope/wrapper. (Speaking of which, some magazines and newspapers sell ad space on their wrappers and also let advertisers insert promotional flyers inside them, for a fee, of course.)

With magazines as with newspapers, there's lots of flexibility, so if you have an unorthodox idea, holler. For example, one publisher agreed to add what we called "tip ins" to his city magazine. He went to his local government employment agency, got the names of people who were looking for work and hired some of them to affix a three-dimensional object to the "run of press" ad we bought in his magazine.

As a result, when readers turned to our ad, they saw copy printed on the page that related to an object that had been glued to the page. One featured the caption, "Have a look," immediately below a photographic slide that readers could remove and look at (it contained our client's sales pitch, of course).

Communications strategists also are interested in where and how magazines are read and how often. How many read a given magazine at home vs. at the doctor's office or on a commuter train? How often are they apt to thumb through it before they discard it? When they're finished, what do they do with it — file it for future reference, throw it out or pass it along?

You may have noticed that each issue of *Reader's Digest* carries as many stories as there are days in the particular month. The publisher's original idea, of course, when he dreamed up the notion way back when, was that this would prompt readers to return to the magazine over and over, every day of the month.

Magazines offer communications strategists selective audiences, complementary editorial environments, creative flexibility (inserts, reply cards, tip-ins, multipage units, gatefolds) and relatively long lead times. Strategists also know that magazine ads typically take two to three weeks to produce.

It's Darwinian

Newspapers become more like magazines, and magazines become more like direct mail, all thanks to the microchip. So what's direct mail becoming more like? It's becoming more like the monster that turns mailboxes into mini-malls.

If your ultimate aims are to deliver a personalized message to a well-defined target audience, direct mail has traditionally been your media vehicle of choice. It's expensive (100 times more costly than newspapers on a per reader basis), but it offers unlimited creative flexibility and is delivered directly to your target audience's mailbox.

Which is where an important problem arises. When your Mr. or Ms. Target Audience gets to the mailbox, he/she is increasingly likely to find that it's filled with solicitations like yours and to toss all of them. The solution: Be distinctive, which is expensive, or use FedEx or UPS, which is extravagant.

If you're a creative communications strategist, it's possible to be distinctive without being extravagant, of course. In fact, that's what you're paid to do. I once discovered a letter from Moscow in my mailbox, Cyrillic characters and all. Intrigued, I opened it immediately only to find a sales pitch for an exercise machine that started out, "Fooled you!" I didn't buy the machine, but I liked the pitch.

For communications strategists, direct mail offers total audience selectivity (if you know your target audience precisely) and tremendous creative flexibility, at a very stiff price.

"I saw it on the radio"

Radio offers lesser degrees of selectivity and creative flexibility less expensively. Radio is cheap in the sense that you can buy a 30-second ad on a local station for as little as $25. However, you won't get as many people for your money as you would if you'd put that $25 toward a newspaper ad or television spot. Of course, if $25 is all you have...

Radio is a background medium. Listeners typically are doing other things while they listen, so your message has to reach out as well as stand out. And you don't have pictures to help you. (You can, however, use sound to create pictures, as we talked about a few chapters ago.)

Nor do you have an accurate approximation of the number of people who hear your messages. Radio audiences are hard to quantify because so many listeners are at work, in their cars, at the beach, etc.

So what attracts communications strategists to radio? Price, of course, but, more importantly, creative possibilities, editorial that speaks to particular audiences (news, classical music, Rush Limbaugh "Dittoheads"), interactivity ("operators standing by") and immediacy. If the air time is available and you're willing to let an announcer deliver your message, you can be on the radio in a matter of hours.

Communications strategists know one other thing about radio, and that's to steer clear of it if the argument or its dramatization is complex. When you have a half-minute or a minute to connect with people who may be driving, typing or sunbathing, your message ought not contain more than two easy-to-grasp points. One's even better.

The boob tube

If technology has caused other media to evolve, it has triggered a revolution on the small screen, one you're quite familiar with, I'm sure. The medium has gone from three networks and a few independent stations to half a dozen networks (with more on the way) and thousands of local stations, on UHF and VHF, plus cable, pay-per-view and satellite TV (whose dishes are now serving-plate size and shrinking). Where will it all end? Who knows?

Television's great appeals to communications strategists are: (1) It offers the combination of sight, sound and motion, so it's the next best thing to a salesperson in every viewer's living room — or bedroom, den, kitchen or workshop, as the case may be — seeing is believing, right?; (2) It provides an opportunity to demonstrate an offering's particular capabilities, much as a salesperson would do if she/he could get into your living room; (3) It reaches lots of people; (4) Those people are paying attention; (5) It offers great creative flexibility — from 10-second reminder messages to 30-minute "infomercials."

Television's drawbacks? (1) Audiences are diverse, not selective, so if you want to reach only women with college degrees, you'll waste a good chunk of your money if you buy television time; (2) Audiences are armed with lethal weapons: remote control devices — which they'll use to zap your message if it isn't instantly riveting; (3) The television landscape is cluttered — huckstering *ad nauseam* — so it's hard to get heard; (4) Television time is expensive; (5) Television ads (mini-movies) are expensive to produce.

A new age

As you know, television, too, is evolving, becoming more PC-like at the same time personal computers are becoming more TV-like.

Cable modems allow you to "watch" the Internet on your television set. And television networks produce news programs designed to be "watched" on personal computers.

All of which is to say that, from a communications strategist's perspective, a new medium has arrived (a "multimedium"). The Internet and its commercial face, the World Wide Web, provide a variety of new and different ways for organizations and individuals to "get heard."

A Web site has become a staple of most communications initiatives, no matter that it's hard to assess the quality of the "hits" it attracts. How much of this fascination with the Web is a passing fancy, a way to appear to be "with it"? Impossible to tell.

Suffice it to say, the Web offers communications strategists a vehicle they can't ignore, especially if they aim to reach younger people who've turned their backs on more traditional media vehicles. The Web not only provides tremendous creative flexibility, it also offers something I think is more important: interactivity. If you're really serious about engaging your target audience in an ongoing dialogue, the Web is the place for you.

Another important consideration: The Web is developing rapidly as a media vehicle. We now have Web magazines ("zines"), radio programs (via software called "Real Audio") and news broadcasts (courtesy of an NBC-Microsoft joint venture). For communications strategists this means, "Pay attention. And stay tuned."

Ubiquity = ?

As you move through your days, you're surely aware of the increasing ubiquity of the media. They've got us surrounded! Your Sunday paper is so full of sales pitches that you risk a hernia when you bend down to pick it up. Your favorite magazine is swollen with ads (a recent issue of *Vogue* ran over 700 pages).

You go to the park, and there are messages on the benches. Look up, and you may see a plane towing a message that implores you to test-drive a Ford. Highways are lined with billboards. Buses and trains are papered with "transit posters." Airplanes offer in-flight magazines, video, audio and catalogs — all including sales pitches, of course.

Public television and, to a lesser degree, public radio beam announcements that are ads in disguise. Your friendly neighborhood supermarket airs "specials" over its PA system ("attention shoppers, don't miss the Velveeta sale on aisle seven"). Even the shopping carts carry mini-billboards.

When will the Law of Diminishing Returns begin to take effect? This is the question for communications strategists. You'll never achieve your communications objective if your voice is lost in an ocean of noise. The price is never right, no matter how inexpensive the medium.

(For doomsayers like me, it should be noted that it was in 1914 that pundit-to-be Walter Lippmann predicted that advertising would soon wither away because it was "a weed that grows because the art of consumption is uncultivated." Don't hold your breath.)

Consider the alternative

Rising noise levels and rising costs for space and time have prompted communications strategists to turn to unconventional "media" to connect with their target audiences. For example:

Trade shows that put representatives face-to-face with target audiences and give them space and time to engage and interact.

Forums, seminars, symposia and *sports events* that feature presentations and discussions of interest to the target audience.

Skytyping, a high-tech twist on skywriting, that employs five planes flying in tight formation that carry computers that have been preprogrammed to trigger the release of blips of smoke at precise intervals. The result: a 25-character message 1,500 feet tall and five miles long.

Pamphleteering. Back to the future; return with us now to those thrilling days of yesteryear; steal a page from Tom Paine's 18th-century playbook; hire kids to hand out your message or stick it on car windshields in places frequented by your target audience. Crude but sometimes effective.

3D billboards. Another new twist on a venerable media vehicle, made possible by advances in the material sciences. Now you can produce a larger-than-life mock-up of your offering or idea (the Jolly Green Giant, say) and attach it to an outdoor advertising board. Pretty spectacular, assuming most of the people who drive by belong to your target audience.

In the highly unlikely event you haven't noticed, I should note that old-fashioned 2D billboards are as ubiquitous as ever. Marketers see them as a "reminder" medium. Copywriters see them as a marvelous medium because it forces them to distill their messages, and because fewer words usually means fewer rewrites.

Kiosks that organizations can erect where target audiences are apt to come across them. They're typically highly involving and interactive. Airports are favored locations.

Video mailings. Now that the cost of duplicating a 10-minute video has dropped below a dollar, it may be cost-effective to tape your message, offer it in ads and then send to respondents. Alternatively, forget the ads, and direct-mail copies of the tape to your target audience cold.

Intel Corp. offered a video of its CEO addressing a major conference in two full-page *Wall Street Journal* ads headlined, "Free Speech." Think about the possible cost. Five million people read the *Journal.* If 1 percent call the toll-free number to request the tape, that's 50,000 tapes to produce, package and ship — not to mention the ad space at $100,000-plus per insertion.

Do you suppose Intel reckoned the strategy would be cost-effective because everyone would see the ads and no one would call for the tape?

I doubt it. I called for — and watched — the tape, and it was most impressive, showed off the CEO and his company in an informative way. The more requests, the better for Intel, I concluded.

Public broadcasting. As public funding shrinks, public television and radio stations increasingly carry underwriting announcements, which, of course, are ads by another name. One company I know spends all its media communications dollars underwriting public radio programs just for the on-air plugs it gets (which its communications director writes). Others will underwrite programs then promote them with "tune-in" ads in newspapers and magazines.

Suffice it to say, as the volume of advertising delivered by traditional media vehicles rises, resourceful communications strategists look for alternatives, even if they have to invent them.

Selection criteria revisited

In chapter one, I touched on five things communications strategists think about when they consider media options. It's worth reviewing them here:

- *Affordability.* A media vehicle may have all the right attributes and be too expensive. Hence, it's important to know how much it costs to use the various vehicles. A client of mine used to say he had Ferrari tastes (when it came to media) and a Volkswagen budget.

- *Reach.* Or coverage. It's essential that the media vehicles you select reach all or nearly all of the people in your target audience. You'll never achieve your communications objective otherwise.

- *Frequency.* Given the competition for people's attention, you need to use whatever media vehicles you choose repeatedly for your message to register with your target audience. How repeatedly? Here are a few rules of thumb:
  - At least three times a month in a daily newspaper.
  - One every six weeks in a weekly magazine.
  - Nine times a year in a monthly.
  - Eighteen spots a week on radio or television.

- *Efficiency.* That is, target audience/dollar. Here's a quiz:
  - *Style* magazine has a circulation of 100,000, 30 percent of whom are in your target audience, and charges $5,000 for a full-page four-color ad.
  - *Verve* magazine has a circulation of 60,000, 65 percent of whom are in your target audience, and charges $6,000 for a full-page four-color ad.

  Which is the more efficient vehicle? (Hint: Focus on the cost per target audience member and you'll learn what the French architect said when he was told, "Less is more"; i.e., "*Mais non,* verve is more.")

- *Context.* That is, how well does the medium fit your message? Does its editorial enhance it? A complementary editorial environment is a big, if incalculable, plus.

Generalizations

If your argument is complex and your audience is educated and middle-aged, think newspapers. If your argument is complex and your audience is very selective, think magazines. If your argument is complex and your audience is young and hip, think Web.

These media vehicles let you take as much space as you need to tell your story, and they let the people in your target audience consider it at their own pace and revisit it as many times as they wish.

If your argument is simple, your audience diverse and your budget ample (circa $10 million), think television. If your budget's not so ample, think radio.

If your time frame is tight, no medium generates awareness as fast as television, but if you need to start communicating "yesterday," radio's the better bet.

Is your argument best portrayed visually? Is sound important? How about motion? If you answered yes three times, you'll be inclined toward television, the Internet or, perhaps, in-flight videos. Just make sure your target audience inclines in the same direction.

I trust this chapter has given you the working knowledge of media attributes you need to be able to juggle cornerstone, copy, art and media considerations in your mind.

The non-media media vehicle

Think of it as a miniature billboard that your target audiences can touch and manipulate and will see at a most opportune time — when they are literally in the market. I'm talking about packaging, of course.

Savvy marketers invest a great deal of time and money in the development of packaging, the result being that packaging has become a quasi-science (and a big business) and packages often cost more than the products inside them. (For example, Pringles potato chips, with their cardboard package that looks like a tennis ball can.)

Package designers pay special attention to materials science, production technologies, environmental laws and customs and in-store settings; that is, how the package is likely to be displayed. All of which leads to some wonderfully artful designs as a stroll down the aisles of any retail store will quickly demonstrate.

As I write, I'm looking at a package for a computer program that teaches kids how to play the piano. My sense is that this package has been designed to be fondled. It offers lots of relevant information succinctly delivered and says, without using the words, "Pick me up, turn me over, read my six panels, and you'll know what you need to know to make an informed decision." It's part spec sheet, part infomercial, very handsome and deftly written.

Package designers also are focusing on the so-called "out of box" experience and are designing user-friendly packages that help people learn how to use their purchases. These packages do double duty: They help buyers and they convert prospects into buyers — by promising to help buyers.

While not a media vehicle per se, packages offer communications strategists timely ways to deliver messages to their target audiences.

Chapter 15

Economies of Scale

Executive Summary

Objective:

Add impact and value (ROI) to your initiative by extending your messages without increasing your budget.

Strategies:

(1) Include a promotions component in your initiative, to stimulate buying activity during slow periods or restart it after a crisis.

A promotion aims to persuade your target audience members to act when you want them to by offering them a special incentive for a limited time.

The best promotions are those that (a) use the idea you've come up with to dramatize your arguments, and (b) promise a lot while costing a little.

There are four types:

- *Premiums* entice buyers by offering them something extra for their money.
- *Deals* promise something for less money.
- *Samples* offer free trials.
- *Sweepstakes* hold out a chance to win some extraordinary thing.

(2) Include a merchandising component in your communications initiative to reinforce your arguments to your target audience.

- "Merchandising" means stretching your basic investment in a campaign idea by developing inexpensive incremental ways to deliver it to your target audience.
- Your point of departure is an inventory of the materials you've produced in the course of readying the primary components of your initiative. You want to reuse this stuff, get it to do double or triple duty.

Please note: When you're producing these materials, don't forget about the merchandising extensions that are to come.

Take that "extra" picture. Have a photographer cover your TV commercial shoots.

- Look for ways to use outtakes.
- Think personal appearances, special events, geegaws, reprints, product placements, co-op programs.
- Work with the media vehicles that are carrying your messages to develop merchandising extensions that serve both of you.

(3) Take a hard look at frequency programs. You can use them to build databases that are extremely valuable if you know how to use them.

(4) Consider developing joint promotions and merchandising programs with other organizations a la fast-food chains and movie producers.

(5) Remember, the best promotions and merchandising programs are usually the result of serious brainstorming. Get your team to focus on these areas.

"Have I got a deal for you!"

I once worked with a CEO who had spent his formative years in the automobile industry. He was a "car guy." One day he was musing about a new product he was high on, and he fell to reminiscing about how it was when you developed a new engine in the car business.

He talked about the moment of truth, which came when you attached a prototype of your new engine to a dynamometer and learned whether it delivered the performance you'd promised on paper. You found out whether, in my client's words, it "made power."

The minute he spoke these words, I glommed on to them. They seemed to me to capture his vision for his company: to supply innovative products that enabled their users to be orders of magnitude more productive — products that "made power."

As soon as I made this connection, he jumped on it, and we had ourselves a dilly of an idea, a pair of words that summed up the company's reason for being.

The question then became, what do we do with them? How do we use them, put them to work, extract as much value from them as we possibly can? In the course of answering these questions, we managed to put "making power" or some variation on every communication to every target audience.

The company's annual report carried a "Making Power" section that described the company's mission. The company's data sheets, brochures, ads, packaging and point-of-sale materials incorporated phrases such as "more power to you" and "System 1000 delivers more power to your people."

The company sponsored "Count the ways…" sweepstakes for customers in each of its markets and employees in each of its divisions.

Each month's employee newsletter featured a CEO-authored "Making Power" column, a "Making Power at…" interview with a division chief that focused on how his/her group came out with products that "made power" for their users, a "Making Power Par Excellence" customer testimonial and a salute to employees who won "Powermaker of the Month" awards.

Human Resources used the theme in its recruiting and employee orientation materials. Plant managers built recognition and incentive programs around it. The CEO tapped it to launch a "Make Power with the Boss" initiative that put him in touch with employees at all levels in informal settings so he could hear what was on their minds.

"Power Makers" became the name of the company's athletic teams. Variations of the theme found their way onto buttons, posters, mugs, glasses, stickers, binders, even license plate frames. Any employee who wanted one could get a frame that said "(company name) makes power" or "(employee name) makes power."

Most important, employees around the world (we translated or interpreted "making power" where we had to) were urged to invent applications and to share their inventions with their colleagues.

In time, the idea took hold, in part because the words had a ring to them and in part because the message was "fully developed" (to say the least!), but mostly because it was both believable and true. The company's products really did "make power." "Making power" really was what the company stood for. And everybody knew it.

I tell this story to illustrate what you can do for very little money to extend a message, idea or theme…if you think about it.

In this chapter, we'll consider two general sorts of message extensions: promotions and merchandising programs.

Promotions

The reasons to invest in promotions are typically to stimulate buying activity during slow periods (Monday nights for restaurants, summer for Florida and the Caribbean) or to restart buying activity after a crisis (product recall, negative story on "60 Minutes").

Their objective is to prompt the people in your target audience to act when you want them to by offering them an argument (incentive) that's external to your product for a limited time.

There are four types of incentives: premiums, deals, samples and sweepstakes. The best incentive is one that extends and exploits the idea you've come up with to dramatize your arguments (e.g., "making power")…and promises a lot while costing a little.

Here are examples of the four types of promotions — drawn from my imagination. Remember the fictional skin-enhancing product I introduced in chapter 10, Dermaglo? Let's resurrect it, and let's say our idea is to hire a popular (among the target audience), middle-aged movie star (we'll call her Sam Magee) to bring Dermaglo to life, make it irresistible.

A **premium** entices buyers by offering them something extra for their money. A Dermaglo premium might feature Sam Magee telling target audience members, "Buy a family pack of Dermaglo by Friday and get a free tote bag to carry it home in."

A **deal** entices buyers by offering them something for less money. A Dermaglo deal might feature Sam Magee alerting target audience members to the fact that they can "save 40 percent on family packs of Dermaglo if they act fast — before 9 p.m. Friday."

A **sample** entices buyers by giving them a free trial. A Dermaglo sampling program might feature mini-packets that (1) show a smiling Sam Magee saying, "Do I have a gift for you!" and (2) include a discount coupon with a 30-day expiration date. These packets could be mailed to target audience members, hung on their front doorknobs or stuck inside the shrink-wrap that protects magazines they buy or subscribe to.

Finally, a **sweepstakes** entices buyers by promising them a shot at the moon; e.g., Sam Magee lets target audience members know that they can "win a weekend for two in Paris via the Concorde just by dropping into any store that offers Dermaglo before 9 p.m. Friday."

Promotions are usually "promoted" via ads, TV spots, radio commercials, mailers, flyers, stuffers and/or point-of-purchase displays.

Again, imagination is the key to success. You want to cook up an offer that promises a lot and costs a little, and this calls for creative thinking, brainstorming, free-associating. Get your team together!

To prime the pump, here are two case histories drawn from my cruise line experience (as opposed to my cranky imagination). Both were responses to rather serious business problems.

Serious problem No. 1

People would book staterooms three or four months in advance of a cruise's departure date, then cancel a month in advance when it came time to make a deposit. This, of course, left the cruise line with an empty stateroom and very little time to fill it.

Our idea was to create a promotional premium that would entice these people *not* to cancel, and to this end we created an elegant "vacation log" that described in glowing, day-by-day detail the experience they were about to have and waxed poetic about the wonderful places to visit at each port of call. It also contained lined pages they could use to record their adventures and log new friends' names and addresses (making new friends being a key motivation).

The log's design picked up the same visual and verbal themes we used in ads, PR and collateral (brochures, shipboard menus, newsletters, etc.). It was a clear extension of the line's overall communications effort. And it was classy! If you saw it, you'd probably guess that each log cost $40 to $50 to produce.

In fact, the unit cost was zero. Indeed, the cruise line made a penny or two each time it sent a log out because the descriptions of the wonderful places to visit at each port of call were ads in disguise. We sold those listings to amortize the log's production and distribution costs.

Incidentally, the cancellation rate dropped 25 percent almost immediately after people started receiving their logs.

Serious problem No.2

Prospects would contact travel agents to inquire about a cruise, and the travel agents would often be unable to help make a booking because they knew very little about the offering. To make matters worse, they had no great interest in learning about it.

We devised a contest to deal with this predicament. Travel agency bosses were invited to enroll their employees in a correspondence course that included six quizzes. The employees who scored highest on these quizzes would win two home entertainment centers — one for themselves and one for their boss.

The invitation also made it clear that the answers to all but six of the quiz questions could be found in the "text booklet" that would be sent to all entrants. So bosses could help their employees if they were so inclined. Each quiz included one essay question that required entrants to fire up their imaginations.

Naturally, the bosses responded enthusiastically, enrolled more than 7,000 of their employees, each of whom received the text booklet, which spelled out the cruise experience quite factually and in considerable detail. Thereafter, for six weeks, they received, completed and returned a quiz a week. The 12 highest scorers won home entertainment centers for themselves and their bosses; all participants earned certificates of graduation.

And why not? They'd learned a great deal about the cruise experience, which they could (and did) use to help their clients decide whether to take a cruise. What's more, the cost of the promotion had been nominal. The text booklet and exams were designed to look "academic" and printed on uncoated paper. And the cruise line "traded out" for the home entertainment centers; that is, they paid for them with staterooms on off-season cruises instead of dollars.

As you can see, well-conceived promotions not only add to the power of your communications initiative at a nominal cost, they also give your organization cost-effective ways to deal quickly with slack periods, slumps and crises.

Merchandising

Back to Dermaglo. We've developed a coherent communications initiative that employs a solid idea (Sam Magee) to dramatize our arguments to our target audience. What more can we do to milk this idea without breaking the budget?

Let's start by taking inventory of what we've paid for. First, we've paid for Sam Magee, which means that, because we anticipated this when we negotiated her contract, we have the option of featuring her at trade shows, conventions, conferences and such special events as we might concoct.

We could send her on a "book tour" to retail stores in key markets, where she could visit with retailers and their customers and talk up the benefits of Dermaglo. We'll photograph these events, of course, and use the pix to publish an attractive booklet for wholesalers, retailers, employees and stockholders, "Travels with Ambassador Sam."

Outtakes

Second, we also have in inventory an array of still photographs of Ambassador Sam with our product, we've filmed and tape-recorded her touting our product and, because we anticipated this moment, we took still photos of her being filmed and tape-recorded touting our product. So we already own a large library of potentially useful materials — materials we can quickly and inexpensively turn into posters, flyers, T-shirts, belt buckles, baseball caps, press releases, mini-movies, etc. Our PR and investor relations people will use them, and Sam, to arrange get-togethers with journalists, security analysts and important institutional investors. Maybe we'll invite Sam to a board meeting, too. The directors would get a kick out of that.

Speaking of movies, perhaps we could sneak a family-size package of Dermaglo into Sam's next film, or, even better, have her take a Dermaglo bath in her next film. Pretty sexy.

Money talk

And then there are all the ads we're running. Each of the publications offers a "merchandising allowance" that we can use in a variety of ways. We'll sit down with the magazines' representatives and concoct programs that work for both of us — starring Sam, natch.

Speaking of ads, how about a co-op program for wholesalers and retailers? We'll provide ad slicks and radio and TV "doughnuts" that feature guess who and an allowance that gives them a financial incentive to use them. We'll use existing photos and footage to make the slicks and doughnuts, so the incremental cost will be next to nothing. (Doughnuts, by the way, are radio and TV spots that have holes in them for retailer identification.)

We might also be able to negotiate joint promotions of Sam's upcoming films with the producing studios. Her agent should be able to help us with that.

How about staging a retrospective of Sam's greatest films? It could travel to key markets. Moviegoers would receive autographed pictures and a free bucket of popcorn — the bucket would, of course, have the Dermaglo logo on the side. Or we could work with a syndicate or cable channel to air the retrospective in major markets, which would allow us to run Dermaglo spots during the breaks.

Enough already!

You have the idea. Once you've invested big bucks in your basic initiative, the add-ons come cheap. The limit isn't your budget; it's your imagination.

One way to stimulate your imagination, by the way, is to check out what others are doing to merchandise their offering, particularly your competitors.

The entertainment industry is worth checking out, including sports franchises. Ditto fast-food providers. They're forever cooking up inventive promotions, often in conjunction with entertainment companies.

A client of mine devised one of my personal favorites. Her company — which we'll call Powerhouse — had silenced a host of naysayers by performing brilliantly in a super-competitive industry, and it had launched a comprehensive marketing communications initiative to tout its success. The theme was, "The Powerhouse Phenomenon," and she was looking for inexpensive ways to extend it.

What she came up with was a company store, which she called "Phenomena." She opened outlets in all the company's facilities and stocked them with "Powerhouse Phenomena," a wide variety of merchandise — pens, pen knives, apparel, office supplies, you name it. Not only did employees patronize these outlets, customers and suppliers did, too, to the point that they made money! Which my client used to help pay for her advertising.

Frequency programs

Or, what's it worth to know your customers' birthdays?

You're familiar with these merchandising programs. You probably belong to one or two of them. The airlines started them, but now everyone's getting in on the act. What about them? Are they worth their considerable cost?

You walk into a restaurant. When you sit down, you notice a tent card on your table inviting you to become a charter member of "Gourmandis Fidelis," a frequent diner program.

Sign up, and you'll get a complimentary baked potato with every meal you consume at this particular establishment, not to mention yet another piece of plastic to go along with your frequent flier cards, your frequent reader card, your frequent car renter card, et. al.

What's going on here? Is Gourmandis Fidelis a good deal? For whom?

The price of a free potato

Let's look at it from the diners' perspective. What do they have to give to get their free baked potatoes? (Remember, there's no such thing as a free baked potato.) Answer: information. About themselves. Bye-bye anonymity. Now their names, addresses, eating habits, drinking habits and tipping habits are known to the operators of the restaurant, as well as the company that handles the restaurant's frequent dining program.

(Another popular variation on this theme: Diners are invited to fill in a card that includes their birth dates as well as their names and addresses in return for a free birthday meal. Restaurateurs use this information to build business on slow nights; e.g., a special mailing to people whose birth dates fall on Mondays).

The return on a free potato

What do restaurant operators get in return for the baked potatoes they give away? In theory at least, greater customer loyalty (which leads to more and better word-of-mouth advertising), increased customer frequency, bigger tabs, fatter tips. But, as I suggested above, the big payoff is data — data that enable them to take the fat out of their marketing and marketing communications programs (no more extravagant mass media campaigns!). Data that allow them to fine-tune their offerings. Data that help them select the best locations for the restaurants they're opening in the months ahead.

Why doesn't everybody do it?

Wow! These really are valuable data, aren't they? And all one has to do to get them is give away a few baked potatoes! What a deal! So why doesn't every restaurant in the world have its version of Gourmandis Fidelis?

Why doesn't every department store, drugstore, hardware, service station, ski resort and supermarket have its version? Macy's or Nothing at All. Safeway Forever. Ace is the Only Place. The Vail Faithful.

How about technology companies ("Best Bytes")? Book publishers ("Not Exactly Random House")? Baked goods providers ("Butternut or Nuttin'")? Health and beauty aid marketers ("Dermaglo Demons")?

Why indeed. There are four reasons: cost, measurability, logistics and what I call quagmire phobia.

Dollars and yardsticks

In fact, the only inexpensive thing about Gourmandis Fidelis is the baked potato. Materials (tent cards, member cards, mailers), data collection and processing systems, training, promotions and postage all carry hefty price tags. And, for most marketers, the only way to afford them is to steal from the ad budget, a nervous-making act.

Of course, these expenses quickly turn into shrewd investments if they produce revenue that more than offsets them, but measuring their return is tricky. It's hard to determine how often Gourmandis Fidelis members frequented the sponsoring restaurant or how much they spent there *before* they signed up.

There are ways out of this box: Ask new members (via surveys) to tell you how often they came before they signed up, test a program in half of your locations and compare revenues, or simply launch a program and assume subsequent revenue increases are attributable to it.

(Marketers who've tested these programs say it takes at least six months to get a reliable fix on their performance.)

The makings of an admin nightmare

Managing a Gourmandis Fidelis program is harder than it looks. Members hand their cards to their waiter, who takes them to the cashier, who swipes them through a card reader, and that's that. However, when there's a line of hungry people waiting for tables, and the cashier is also the hostess, and the waiter has a party of eight whose chicken fricassees are getting cold out in the kitchen, a simple-sounding procedure can become a pain in the, ah, elbow.

And, of course, there are tent cards, mailers and membership cards to order, design, print and distribute, records to keep, new employees to train, old employees to reinvigorate, data to keep clean and current and to analyze — often at 3 a.m. The logistics can be daunting…and sleep-depriving.

Quagmire ahead?

And then there's the quagmire factor, the fear that — like movies on airplanes and cable TV in hotel rooms — frequency programs will become so widespread that marketers will have to offer them to avoid losing business.

Remember credit cards. Once marketers could choose not to accept "all major credit cards," they could require their customers to pay cash, but not anymore. Credit cards have become ubiquitous. Are frequency programs right behind them? And, if so, what's a poor marketer to do? Hold out? Or move quickly to put a program in place ahead of the competition?

Be creative

For communications strategists who believe with me that Albert Einstein was right when he said, "Imagination is more important than knowledge," there's a third option. Take an off-the-shelf program and make it special, dress it up, customize it. Invent ways to make it more appealing to customers, invent ways to collect additional useful data and invent ways to make better use of the data you collect.

Here you have a marketing challenge (add customer appeal) and a technical challenge (squeeze more value out of the information you're collecting). How to respond? Gather your marketing, communications and database management people around your conference (or dining room) table, give them plenty of coffee, colas, sandwiches, salads, cookies and sweet rolls and tell them to go crazy.

But not too crazy. They need to focus their craziness on the practical, strive for conceptions that are both magnificent and useful. Like United Airlines does.

Oh, those friendly skies

I'll put myself through all sorts of contortions to fly United, thanks almost entirely to its frequent-flier program. I'll make intermediate stops. I'll spend longer in the air. I'll delay my departure. I'll pay more. Which is to say, I know firsthand the power of frequency programs.

How has United managed to clasp this very frequent flier (circa 125,000 miles/year) so tightly to its corporate bosom? Not by doling out "plus miles," oddly enough. No, United hooked me with baked potatoes I can use every day; to wit:

- I can reserve exit-row seats (with their extra leg room) in advance via a special "1K" toll-free number that almost never requires me to "hold for the next available operator."
- I can board with first-class passengers so I never have to fight for scarce overhead bin space.
- I'm backed up automatically when delays threaten my connections.
- I'm given uncrowded, well-appointed places to work in many of the airports I frequent ("1K Clubs"), as well as perks that come "out of the blue" — a thank-you letter with a bunch of first-class upgrade certificates, for example.

United once sent me a notice that listed employment opportunities and invited me to nominate worthy candidates. How's that for an imaginative perk? I nominated my son.

In return for all these baked potatoes, I not only fly United all over the place, I also give them all sorts of information about me.

The new dimension

Concentrating on the practical may lead your brainstormers to what I see as the most valuable dimension of a frequency program: *the chance it offers to initiate substantive dialogues with key customers.* It can deliver what up-to-date marketers prize: genuine, real-time interactivity.

You no longer have to run an ad with a toll-free number or a coupon, then sit back and wait hours, days, weeks for feedback from customers, prospects and kooks. Now, in return for a baked potato or two, you can write, call, fax and/or e-mail particular customers and groups of customers, and commence dialoging…and learning.

How do the people Bob Smith serves evaluate his performance? What do those who ordered the new vegetarian scramble think of it? What other entrees would they like to see on the menu? What other restaurants do 25-percent tippers favor? Why? What sorts of premiums would prompt weekend diners to come in on Mondays?

How do Dermaglo Demons rate three alternative formulations? Is it worth 10 percent more than the Dermaglo they use now? No? Then what would make it worth 10 percent more?

Putting customers to work

This is powerful stuff, no matter what kind of business you're in, and frequency programs make it feasible. Your customers can literally join your marketing, advertising, public relations and database management people at your conference table. You can tap directly into their imaginations, stimulate them to think on your behalf. They start working for you. The cliché, "customer intimacy," takes on a whole new meaning.

Technology, of course, promotes this intimacy. As "neural networks" (that scan databases for patterns) and networked PCs become more pervasive, frequency programs become more valuable.

This may be the most compelling reason for communications strategists to pay attention to frequency programs. Increasingly powerful and pervasive digital technologies will make it easier to administer these programs and to interact with precisely defined customer groups.

You can "chat" with a selection of Gourmandis Fidelis members online.

An April fools joke?

In its April 1, 1995, issue, *The Economist* magazine reported on the "expensive ineffectiveness of marketing." It opined that "advertising has become more expensive and less effective as media outlets have proliferated and their audience has fragmented," and held up database marketing programs such as Gourmandis Fidelis and Mileage Plus as an attractive alternative.

The Economist has it right. Its issue date notwithstanding, the power of these programs and their impact on communications deserve to be taken seriously. They fit the times, our "Interactivity Age."

A question for your CFO

Given that an investment in a frequency program will produce revenue for many, many years, is it a mistake to measure its ROI annually? Does our propensity to think in annual terms blind us to the true worth of this investment?

Suffice it to say, an investment United Airlines made in 1983 has generated incremental purchases by me ever since — and presumably will continue to do so until one or the other of us flies into the friendly skies of eternity. How in the world does one calculate the return on this investment? How does one judge its true worth?

When you're planning your communications initiative, you might want to talk with your financial people about this; ask them to spread the cost of this merchandising component over five or 10 years. It will make it easier to achieve your objectives.

Kissing cousins

Promotion and merchandising are kissing cousins that can complement each other and strengthen your initiative as a consequence. So get your team to brainstorm them together.

Need a model? Fast food/movie tie-ins. They promote; i.e., they build business at restaurants and theaters by offering incentives during the time the movie is playing. And they merchandise; i.e., they extend the campaign idea with a gazillion geegaws — Batman straws, Ronald McDonald discount movie coupons, what have you.

Chapter 16

Your Turn

"Over to you."

It's time for a change of pace. Time for you to shift gears and exercise your creativity. In this chapter, I'll give you a skeletal marketing communications assignment, then leave it to you to cook up a set of irresistible communications strategies — with a little help from me in the form of leading questions and free associations.

Here's your assignment:

MIDNIGHT MARCOM
Work Order

Client: Gillette

Product: Ponce de Leon Skin Spray (PdL)

Assignment: Design a marketing communications program for a 12-week market test beginning April 1 in Indianapolis to introduce this revolutionary product.

- Creative, media, merchandising, sales promotion and public relations strategies.
- $3.2 million test budget, enough to finance high-impact communications schedules.

Situation: Research has determined that 50 percent of all men between the ages of 40 and 65 (25 million men, nationally) are very concerned about facial wrinkles.

Gillette has responded by formulating PdL, a combination after-shave and skin tightener. It's applied like after-shave, smells like after-shave and tightens facial skin sufficiently to remove wrinkles for 24 hours.

The tightening process (patented) typically takes about 10 minutes.

One $15 bottle will last two weeks when used daily. There is no other product like it on the market.

Testing has found that the product works and users like it very much. They are, however, extremely reluctant to acknowledge that they're concerned about facial wrinkles.

In one series of focus groups, several men described a product that removed facial wrinkles as "for sissies."

The challenge is to introduce PdL in a way that overcomes this objection. Users want the product; they're simply reluctant to admit it — to others and to themselves.

And admission must precede trial.

Research also found that women would consider buying a wrinkle-removing skin spray for men they knew intimately.

Objective: Trial and one repeat purchase. PdL will be carried by all major supermarket, drug and discount chains and department stores in metro Indianapolis. The test will be considered successful if 40,000 bottles are sold over the 12-week period.

Gillette expects that 10 percent of the 250,000 men between the ages of 40 and 65 who live in metro Indianapolis will try PdL, and that two-thirds of the men who try it will either buy, or acquiesce in the purchase of, a second bottle.

Requirement: The strategies must mesh. It must be clear to the target audiences that the same "voice" is speaking at all times in all communications — advertising, merchandising, sales promotions, packaging, point-of-purchase, public relations, skytyping, what have you.

Questions/free associations

- Among all the men and women in the defined age group who could purchase PdL, who are most likely to do so?

- How would you define, characterize and personify this "best prospects" group — demographically, psychographically and attitudinally?

- Should your target audience definition distinguish between purchasers and users? How about purchase influencers? How much weight will you assign to the three groups?

  Do wives, girlfriends, women friends, mothers, dermatologists, barbers and close professional associates matter? How much?

  How likely is it that Charlie's boss or law firm partner will take him aside and whisper, "Do yourself and our outfit a favor; try Ponce de Leon skin spray?"

- The arguments to all three groups — assuming you decide there are three groups — are straightforward. What's tricky is how and where to dramatize them.

- Don't forget to make it clear in all communications that Gillette isn't just introducing a new product, it's introducing a new kind of product. There has never been anything like PdL before, and there is nothing else like PdL now.

- How do you propose to "make the case" to each group?

- What is your irresistible campaign idea?

- What media do you propose to use to deliver this idea?

- Should there be one idea (or theme), or is it better to employ a different idea for each target audience?

- Is there a single media vehicle that reaches the target audience(s) efficiently, effectively and comprehensively?

- How about humor? Can it overcome the sensitivities revealed by research? A John Wayne-type poking fun at himself? "Of course I use PdL. Because I gotta look at myself in the mirror at least once a day." Burt Reynolds? Bruce Willis?

- How about irony? Satirize other promotions for similar products; e.g., Rogaine, men's perfumes and hair colorings, women's beauty aids. A little irreverence, an iconoclastic touch, could get lots of attention — if it's flawlessly executed.

- Or, "It's time to face the music," and "the music" is PdL?

- How about a straight-from-the-shoulder, no-nonsense, "man-to-man" appeal? Jack Palance saying, "Face it, men. None of us is getting any younger, and our faces tell the tale."

- How about an anecdotal human-interest approach a la Procter & Gamble's notorious "slice of life" ads that filled radio and television airwaves for four decades? (See sidebar.)

  For example: We see four middle-aged golfers in action. One uncorks a drive that prompts one of his mates to whisper to another, "What's gotten into Harry? He's hitting his drives farther than he has in years." The reply: "He's built up his self-confidence."

  Another possibility: the Charlie and his boss/partner vignette I hypothecated earlier.

- Can something be made of PdL's April 1 intro date? "This is no April Fool's joke."

- How about live product demonstrations on TV, either in ads ("Live from the Hoosier Dome…") or on local programs? Viewers see Mr. Smith applying the product in a live 30-second TV spot at 10:06 a.m. and showing off its effects in another live 30-second TV spot at 10:16 a.m.

- How about in-store demos? Or midday demos in places where there's a lot of pedestrian traffic?

- How about time-lapse photography as the basic idea? It works in all media, but maybe it's too graphic. Do the target audiences want to see how it happens?

- Does it make sense to offer samples given its steep price?

- What about staging a festive, tongue-in-cheek "beauty" contest — with real and apparently valuable prizes, of course. It would certainly get the community's attention. Would it also alienate some of your more straightlaced target audience members?

- How about giving away specially designed hand mirrors as a merchandising extension? It would carry the PdL logo and the line, "Would PdL help? You decide." Such a mirror, with this line, could also be the basis of an ad campaign.

- How about tie-ins with men's stores, or the men's furnishings departments of the department and discount stores that have agreed to carry PdL? "Buy a new suit and get a bottle of PdL free."

- How about tying to the season, given that the test coincides with spring, and spring being a time of renewal, "thoughts of love," blossoming, baseball, etc.?

- How about tying in with Gillette razors and shaving cream? "Buy a bottle of PdL and we'll throw in a Sensor razor and a can of Foamy."

- Should we do some pretesting? Do we need to make sure our arguments square with our target audience's concerns? Do we want to get reactions to a few alternative campaign ideas? How, given concept testing's Achilles heel? (See sidebar.)

- Public relations is critical. You want PdL to be the biggest, best, most enjoyable and most visible thing ever to make it to Indianapolis.

  You want every Hoosier in the market discussing, debating, poking fun at PdL in every forum. Elementary schoolteachers and university philosophy professors talk with their students about whether it's a good or bad thing for their dads to use PdL.

Couples argue about PdL over the breakfast table; neighbors debate it over the back fence. Priests, ministers and rabbis sermonize about it. The media have a field day.

At least, this is your dream. How will you make it come true? How will you interest metro Indianapolis journalists and public figures in writing and talking about PdL and its impact on the community?

Is an event, like a beauty contest, the way to go?

Could the governor or the General Assembly (Indiana's legislature) be persuaded to designate the first week of April "Be Nice to Your Face Week"? Would a few campaign contributions or a donation to a popular local cause do the trick?

Should a panel of doctors be convened under Gillette's aegis to talk about PdL's health dimensions ("the poor man's Prozac")?

PdL is a PR person's dream…and a PR person's nightmare, a revolutionary product and an unrevolutionary community. Be creative. Be strategic (i.e., make sure PR meshes with all other marketing communications). Be careful.

Concept testing done right

The campaign's objective was to convince opinion leaders that the sponsor was a "responsible outfit." We and our client had come up with four arguments, and we wanted to see which had the greatest appeal to the target audience.

We created six scrapbooks that contained unsigned, unstylized visual/verbal representations of the four arguments, then hired six researchers to show these scrapbooks to target audience members. They made appointments by phone, then visited respondents in their homes.

Their visits were brief. They asked only one question: "I'm about to hand you a scrapbook with statements from four manufacturing companies — the Smith Co., the Jones Co., the Hill Co. and the Valley Co. All four of these companies would like to build a plant in your community. Only one will be allowed to. Would you please review their statements and then tell me which one you would prefer?"

This question got to the heart of "responsibility" and yielded a clear winner. We developed four creative expressions of it and repeated the test. Same methodology, same single question. Same result: another clear winner.

At this point, we were confident enough to run a tight prototype of the winner in the St. Louis metro edition of *Newsweek* and then to interview *Newsweek* subscribers in St. Louis who belonged to our target audience by phone. We measured recall, comprehension and impressions against norms supplied by the research company and our own historical experience.

This yielded more evidence that the campaign was a winner. Recall, comprehension and impression scores were twice the norms and well above our historical experiences. As a result, we were able to launch the campaign across the nation with confidence and to demonstrate to top management that we had done so only after careful consideration and examination.

The time and money involved in these steps were considerable ($75,000 and three-plus months), but, viewed in light of the stakes (large national budget, the CEO's authority), they were well worth taking.

Concept testing done wrong

Everybody loved the idea. From CEO to assistant media planner, we all knew intuitively that we had a winner. There was only one problem.

To implement the idea, we would have to produce an exceedingly expensive television commercial.

The CEO agonized, "Should I trust my gut or cover my backside?" and finally decided that we couldn't risk spending the money until we had solid evidence that the idea was as powerful as we all felt it was.

So, at the ad manager's request (and over our objections), we produced an animatic of the commercial (a series of stills on tape) and showed it to six focus groups. The results were so frustrating that, after one group, the CEO (who attended all of them) emerged from behind the one-way glass to engage the participants directly.

The source of his and our frustration: the fact that the people in the focus groups either didn't get the idea or chose not to acknowledge that they'd gotten it to strangers, and we didn't know which was the case.

We decided that it was the research method, not the idea, that was unsound, and we scheduled a series of one-on-one interviews with target audience members. Same basic approach: show the animatic, then ask about comprehension and impressions. Once again, responses were all over the lot, to the point that the psychologist who conducted the interviews said her own method was wrong.

She argued that the idea as communicated by the commercial was so unusual and so personal that many of the people she interviewed were either unable or unwilling to acknowledge their reactions to it to someone they didn't know. She, too, felt that nearly everyone got it, but many weren't able to articulate what they got.

In other words, the idea had hooked her just as it had the rest of us professionals.

After spending a bunch of money and time, we still didn't have objective evidence of the idea's power — or lack of power — because most people are simply unable to articulate, on the basis of one artificial exposure, how they react emotionally to a communication they've never seen before. And, of course, the more unconventional the communication, the greater the likelihood of this.

This is copy testing's Achilles heel and the reason our CEO finally threw up his hands and said, "To hell with testing. Let's roll the dice." Too bad there aren't more CEOs like him around.

Happy ending: The dice came up winners. The campaign did everything it was supposed to and a whole lot more.

A communications strategy writ large

I referred to Procter & Gamble's notorious "slice of life" radio and television ads in one of this chapter's free associations. They were often ridiculed for being "flatfooted" and ham-handed." They never won awards for creativity and artistry. But they helped move a whole lot of merchandise for four decades.

Other marketers imitated and satirized them, but none achieved the degree of consistency and uniformity that P&G did. Every communication for every product followed the same formula. It was — and is — a perfect example of a communications strategy writ large.

The formula? It can be stated in three words: problem, solution, results. Open with a problem you know your target audience frets about ("ring around the collar"). Demonstrate that the product solves the problem better than rivals. Close with proof of the solution and the elation it causes.

Sound familiar? It should. P&G's formula is now pushing 70, but it's alive and well and still widely used…in disguise. Today's marketers have cloaked it with humor. Mr. Whipple ("Don't squeeze the Charmin") isn't supercilious anymore; he's funny. The waitress who cleans up the mess (Bounty) is a well-known comedienne. Savvy marketers realize that there's nothing like wit to add entertainment value and make the incredible credible.

Chapter 17

Now We Don Our Great Black Robes

Executive Summary

Objective:

Develop a procedure to evaluate your communications' aesthetic appeal.

Strategies:

(1) Recognize — and persuade your colleagues who have a say in evaluating the style of your organization's communications to recognize — that:

- Style is subjective by definition. One person's masterpiece is another's fish wrap.

- This subjectivity extends to your target audience. No matter what you do, some won't cotton to its aesthetics.

    The goal is not unanimity, which leads to blandness, but rather maximum involvement and engagement.

    You want your communications to engage and inspire as many members of your target audience as possible without alienating the rest.

(2) Don't make style decisions by committee or consensus. Don't appoint an aesthetics czar. Do use the three-step procedure I'm about to suggest.

(3) Step one: Parse the communication under your microscope and score it on a 1-10 scale vis-à-vis these criteria:

- The clarity and completeness of its *copy structure* (see chapter 10 for a definition).

    That is, how well does the headline attract? How well does the body make the case? How well does the close explain the action you want your target audience to take?

- The power and appropriateness of its *copy style* (chapter 10).

    That is, how readable is it? How involving? How appropriate, given the nature of the arguments?

- The stopping power and communicating power of its *visualization* (see chapter 11 for a definition).

   That is, its ability to stop your target audience in its collective tracks and to deliver at least the beginnings of your argument.

- The stopping power and appropriateness of its *layout* (chapter 11).

   That is, its ability to attract your target audience and lead its collective eye through your message.

(4) Step two: Score the communication as a whole on a 1-10 scale according to how well it answers these questions:

- How distinctive is it?
- How interesting is it?
- How succinct is it?
- How personal is it?
- How credible is it?

(5) Step three: Double the score you gave the communication for its credibility.

(6) You now have 10 scores. Add them and if the total is less than 85, call for a rethink.

"The headline should be bigger." "The background should be tan."
"The boss will never go for that green tint." "What will his wife say?"

You know the drill. A Suit and a Martian with green hair present a spiffy brochure layout to a group that includes you and four colleagues. Then they leave and the fun starts.

"Well," you say, "what do you think?"

"The headlines should be bigger."

"The copy from page two belongs under the picture on page three."

"The lawyers will never let us italicize our warranty."

"Charlene (the CEO's wife) won't go for the funny type on the cover. And besides, she doesn't like green." (Referring to the layout, not the Martian's hair.)

How many times have you heard comments like these? How often have you said to yourself, "Whatever happens to this brochure (or ad, A/V script or press release), it will happen for the wrong reasons. We've got to figure out a better way to evaluate creative work"?

But what is this "better way"?

Copy testing? It's artificial and, unless you're prepared to spend a bundle, the sample sizes will be too small to base aesthetic decisions on.

While copy testing can tell you whether you're getting your arguments across, it can't give you a good fix on your communication's stopping power. Nor can it tell you much about how it's causing people to feel — the emotional connection it makes.

And, as you know, it's this emotional connection that separates communications that get heard from the far more numerous also-rans. It's what we pay green-haired Martians to create.

So what are the options? Pass the buck to the CEO (and his/her spouse)? Form yet another committee (to indulge in what a friend calls "group grope")? Give one person the final say on all style issues, so once everyone signs off on what is said (the argument), this person decides how it gets said?

Number three looks pretty good on paper, but, in practice, being aesthetics czar is a thankless (and often dead-end) job given the infernal subjectivity of it all. (You make everybody mad at you.)

Better to do two things

First, recognize that the "infernal subjectivity of it all" extends beyond your outfit's walls — all the way to your target audience.

Second, set up an evaluation procedure that minimizes it (i.e., subjectivity).

We who sit in meetings and make knowing observations about typography, photography and mixed metaphors may not like to admit it, but when it comes to matters of style, no matter where we end up, some of the folks in our target audience won't cotton to it.

An illustration or turn of phrase that gives you and me goosebumps will go unappreciated by one or another of the perspicacious men and women we aim to sell our widgets to. Don't forget there are people who yawn while looking at Michelangelo's Pieta and prefer lawn bowling to golf and tennis.

Incidentally, this truth, when it's recognized by those who have a say in a communication's aesthetics, can be a leavening agent in style discussions. Put it on the table next time a colleague holds forth passionately on the nuances of *sans serif* type and see how quickly humility sets in and the temperature drops.

Fact is, stylistic subjectivity offers communications strategists an opportunity. We can do what Coca-Cola does. We can change our tunes, beam out sales pitches in a variety of styles and so persuade people of differing tastes — all of whom are in our target audience.

It's no accident that Baskin-Robbins offers 31 flavors and Heinz markets 57 varieties. Our target audiences are no more of one mind than our colleagues are.

A contradiction?

Let's see if I can read your mind. You're thinking that I've just contradicted myself. After beating the drums of consistency and coherence for 16 chapters, here I go advocating inconsistency and incoherence.

I plead not guilty. And I offer Coca-Cola's marketing communications as Exhibit A in my defense. It's certainly true that they're stylistically different, but it's also true that they're "always" (sorry, couldn't resist) recognizably Coca-Cola's. Stylistic consistency underlies stylistic differences.

It's a three-ring circus with one very recognizable master of ceremonies.

(We once created a successful program for a client that included as one of its communications strategies "be consistently inconsistent"; that is, surprise the target audience so consistently that surprise becomes the stylistically unifying thread.)

A procedure

I'm about to offer you a simple three-step way to evaluate the style of your communications. But first, a caveat: It won't work until everyone who uses it agrees on the cornerstone definitions.

Given this agreement, we can take the first step, which is to divide style into four components, then use each as an evaluation criterion.

Step two is to evaluate the communication according to five general criteria ("commandments," I call them).

Step three shall remain a mystery for the moment. Stay tuned.

Step one: the elements of style

There are four, and you've already met them, in chapters 10 and 11: *copy structure, copy style, visualization* and *layout*. Now it's time to use these elements that helped you create your communications to help you judge them.

First, is there a clear *copy structure?* How effectively does each component (head, body, close) do what it's supposed to do? Will the head stop a busy member of your target audience and prompt him/her to say, "I'd better check this out"?

Does the body make the case clearly? Does the close communicate explicitly and unmistakably what you want the target audience to do?

Once you've answered these questions, you'll find it easy to score the communication under your microscope in terms of its copy structure. I suggest that you use a 1-10 scale because it will enable you to easily combine the scores you give each style element into an overall rating.

When you evaluate your communication's *copy style*, remember that the issue is appropriateness; that is, how well does it accord with your arguments and your organization's character and how likely is it to appeal to your target audience? Your answers will determine your scores.

The key questions in scoring your communication's *visualization* are: How compelling is it? How informative? How telegraphic? And how closely does it tie to the headline?

When you score your communication's *layout*, the questions I suggest you ask are: How effectively will its design catch your target audience's eye (and ear)? How smoothly will it lead this collective eye through your story? And how well does it support your arguments?

That is, if one of your arguments is reliability, and the designer has used three typefaces and four type sizes to display the headline, you've got a Whoops! Mark it down. Way down.

Also — and this is an important and underrated issue — how easy will it be for your target audience to read the copy? If 80 percent of your target audience wear bifocals and the type size for the copy is nine point, Whoops!

However, type size isn't this issue's only dimension. Typeface is almost as important. Some faces are designed to be read (the preferred choice of newspapers) others to be admired (the preferred choice of some designers). Do you want people to admire your communication or read it?

We've completed step one; we've put your communication under the microscope and scored it in terms of its elements of style — as if we were judges at a diving competition. On to step two.

Step two: the commandments

Time to look at your communication in its entirety, ask five questions about it, then use our 1-10 scale to express your answers. The five questions are:

- How distinctive is it?
- How interesting is it?
- How succinct is it?
- How personal is it?
- How credible is it?

How distinctive? Your communication aims to stop, interest and persuade people who see and hear hundreds of communications every day and tune out just about all of them.

Will yours be one of the handful that register? If so, will it register that it's yours and not one of your rivals? If you cover the logo, could it be a competitor's communication?

The ultimate in distinctiveness, of course, is the communication that's identifiable even when its logo is covered. When we see cupped hands, we think Allstate. Cowboys on the range, Marlboro. These get "10s" for distinctiveness. They also set a standard we can use when we score ours.

(How often have you heard someone rave about a TV spot, then either misidentify or be unable to recall the sponsor? How often have you been this someone? Clearly, the ad you enjoyed failed to distinguish itself in your mind. If you were a member of the target audience, it was a waste of money as far as you were concerned.)

How interesting? As I've said before (perhaps too often), we live in a time of expanding information flows and contracting attention spans. As a consequence, your communications need to be more interesting than ever — as gripping as a Stephen King novel, as riveting as a Martin Scorcese film — or else.

If they're just "pretty interesting," they're a waste of money. On a 1-10 scale, they get a zero. "Gripping" and "riveting" get 9.5s.

How succinct? You're busier and more stressed out than you've ever been, right? And so is everybody else. Chaos reigns. So your communications must be telegraphic, which, by the way, does not mean short. If it takes 5,000 words to make your case, so be it. Just check to be sure every word is relevant. And score accordingly.

How personal? As I've said (too often?), target audiences aren't groups. They're collections of individuals. They're your cousin Michael and my neighbor Jane. Effective communications talk with their target audiences like you and I talk with Michael and Jane.

So the people in our target audiences say to themselves, "This brochure speaks to me!" Decide how well your communications "speak to me," and score accordingly.

How credible? As we cope with more information from more sources, we get more skeptical of everything. It's not enough for communications to be truthful, they also have to be credible. Are yours?

For better or worse, credibility is more important than truth, perceptions being the coin of the realm here. So judge harshly. Put yourself in the shoes of the most skeptical member of your target audience. Ask yourself, "Will he/she believe this communication?" And score it accordingly.

Step two, then, consists of evaluating and scoring the communication under your scrutiny vis-à-vis five more criteria. We now have nine, and we're about finished. All that's left is step three.

Step three: the double whammy

The envelope please. Step three is double the score you gave to the fifth question in step two, how credible? Now, the perfect communication scores 100 points. Ten "10s." This is what we're all shooting for.

Erect a high standard

The chief executive officer of a successful engineering firm is reputed to have said something I resonate to: "Winning is easy. It's being perfect that's hard."

You're planning to invest a lot of money in your communications initiative. You'll add your messages to the glut. And, if they're not darn near perfect, your target audience will ignore them. So don't compromise. There's no such thing as a stylistically "OK" or "so-so" communication. There are nines, 10s and failures — As, B+s and Fs.

So if you tote up your scores and the total is less than 85, call for a rethink. From an aesthetic point of view, you haven't got a message that's worth putting your organization's money behind.

A Useful, Enjoyable Exercise

Invite each of your colleagues who review your outfit's marketing communications with you (including the people who create them) to get a copy of the same magazine and to pick the one ad in it that they deem to be the most effective (using the scorecard below). Then get together over sandwiches to discuss — and defend — your choices. You'll have a good time, and you'll learn something about each other's tastes.

The Scorecard

	Hall of Shame			Dubious Achievement					Hall of Fame	
	1	2	3	4	5	6	7	8	9	10
Copy Structure	__	__	__	__	__	__	__	__	__	__
Copy Style	__	__	__	__	__	__	__	__	__	__
Visualization	__	__	__	__	__	__	__	__	__	__
Layout	__	__	__	__	__	__	__	__	__	__
Distinctiveness	__	__	__	__	__	__	__	__	__	__
Interest	__	__	__	__	__	__	__	__	__	__
Succinctness	__	__	__	__	__	__	__	__	__	__
Personal-ness	__	__	__	__	__	__	__	__	__	__
Credibility (Double this score)	__	__	__	__	__	__	__	__	__	__

Overall Score: _____

Chapter 18

Naming the Baby

"Ain't science wonderful?"

The CEO had remade the company through a series of shrewd acquisitions, divestitures and financial maneuvers, to the point that its hallowed name had become a misnomer. We were called in to find a moniker that fit.

The CEO said he didn't much care what the name was as long as it was "short, sweet and simple." In fact, his preferred solution was simply to turn the company's three letter stock symbol into its name.

But his investor relations vice president was of a different mind, and she persuaded him that we could come up with an innovative name that would help them win over institutional investors.

We, of course, approached the assignment like the good strategists we were: We set out a procedure, gained endorsement of it from all interested parties, read and read some more, interviewed securities analysts, portfolio managers, financial journalists and employees of the acquired companies.

A Peterbilt or a Dusenberg?

We then drafted a questionnaire to be filled out by the CEO and his eight-person brain trust prior to our interviewing them. Its stated objectives were (1) to elicit respondents' feelings about the company's mission and character, and (2) to focus and energize follow-on interviews. Here are a few sample questions:

- Does Nuco have a sense of humor? If so, what sort? Is it the sarcastic wit of a Don Rickles, the wisecracking wit of a Johnny Carson, the self-deprecating wit of a Garrison Keillor, the gentle wit of a Will Rogers, the outlandish wit of a Gary Larson, or is it something else?

- Is Nuco a parent working lovingly to ready his/her children to fend for themselves, a professor working disinterestedly to ready his/her students to fend for themselves, or a football coach working enthusiastically to ready his players to win a league championship?

- Which of these vehicles best symbolizes Nuco — Ferrari, Volvo, Toyota, Cadillac, Peterbilt, Land Rover, Dusenberg or Corvette?

- If you could write the *Wall Street Journal*'s boilerplate description of Nuco (25 words or less), what would you write?

The questionnaire also asked respondents to score 19 characteristics/attributes/qualities on a 1-10 scale in terms of their relevance to Nuco (e.g., "the ability to quickly evaluate potential investments in Southeast Asia").

Once the brain trusters had completed this questionnaire (which they all did enthusiastically, by the way), we interviewed each of them individually, then brought them together for a free-form, freewheeling discussion/brainstorming session.

What's in a letter?

Unlike children, corporate and product names are meant to be seen and heard, so how they look and sound are key criteria; and when it comes to looks, individual letters — and combinations of letters — matter. Some are simply better looking than others.

Take TOYOTA, for example. The four letters used in this name are not only easy on the eye and ear, they have something else going for them — something quite dramatic. Can you see it? All four are symmetrical. They look the same in your rear-view mirror as they do through your windshield.

Too bad the brand name isn't ATOYOTA — a visual, verbal palindrome!

Eureka!

At this point, something unusual happened: An obvious solution manifested itself ("But of course, why didn't I think of that?"): Nuco should simply take the name of its key acquisition. The latter company had a name that was widely known and respected and a reputation that was exactly what the Nuco execs aspired to.

Sadly, neither the CEO nor his investor relations director felt comfortable with this solution, for "political reasons." ("It just wouldn't look right.") So we established nine criteria, created a scorecard to "objectify" the process and started list-building.

The scorecard had 11 columns. The first was headed "candidate names," two through 10 carried the nine criteria at the top and 11 carried the heading "total." Scorers rated each candidate name on a 1-10 scale according to how well it met each criterion, then toted up their ratings to get a composite score.

Candidate	Distinctive	Accurate	Memorable	Tolerable	Credible	Easy to say/hear	Handsome	Infers a benefit	Protectable	Total
Apex										
Sage										
Upside										
Just So										

Eureka II

We were in the midst of list-building when the investor relations director invited me to one of the briefings the company often gave to institutional investors. While listening to the CEO talk informally about the company to this small and sophisticated group, I got what I thought was a really good idea. I shared it with my hostess (the investor relations director), and she agreed to let me try it out on the CEO the next afternoon. His reaction was instantaneous: "I buy it."

But then the plot thickened. The investor relations director tried to talk her boss out of the name he'd just bought, said it was too long, proposed to test it against other candidates in a series of focus groups. He shrugged, said he was perfectly happy with the name he'd just heard, but he'd go along with some testing if she insisted.

She did. And as we prepared for the focus groups, it became apparent why. She had her own favorite, a name she'd been carrying in her hip pocket for half a year, the name of one of the company's divisions.

Despite the fact that the name the CEO had "bought" was well-received by partici-pants in the focus group interviews, she was able to convince him to go along with her name by arguing that it would save time and money because the company already owned it.

So a project that consumed almost a year turned out to be irrelevant, a waste of a lot of time, simply because the investor relations director felt she needed to go through all the motions to end up where she wanted to be at the start.

The ultimate irony, however, was yet to come: Two years later, a new CEO and his consorts grew tired of her name and decided to do what we proposed at the beginning of the project. They took the name of their key acquisition.

Projects from hell

There are two communications projects that typically begin with all parties expressing their commitment to orderly procedures and then rather quickly lurch into chaos. The first I've just illustrated — naming/renaming products, services or enterprises. The other is annual reports.

If you've worked on an annual, you know what I mean. If not, steer clear. Annual reports have so many masters — management, finance, legal, investor relations, marketing — that it's darn near impossible to write a coherent one, unless, of course, you're able to do what Warren Buffett does.

Buffett, chief executive officer of Berkshire Hathaway and a legend in his own time, simply writes his company's annual report himself. No "ghosts." No departmental reviews. Just Buffett, pure and unadulterated. Pictures are few and far between. Breast-beating, the bane of so many annuals, is nonexistent. It reads like a personal letter from a good friend.

Small wonder that, year in and year out, Berkshire-Hathaway's annual report is the best read (in both senses of the word). It's intelligent, informative, coherent and interesting. If I were a captain of industry, I'd try to hire Buffett to write my annual reports, and if he wouldn't, I'd tell my communications people to copy his approach shamelessly and acknowledge the imitation on page one.

How to minimize the madness that surrounds annual report production? I offer these suggestions:

- Start early, publish a realistic timetable and estimate the financial consequences of falling behind (e.g., overtime, which typically doubles printing costs).
- Interview the masters individually and then together, as we did with Nuco's brain trust, and get them to agree on the ground rules, a.k.a. situation and cornerstones.

  In my experience, most annual report madness arises from disagreements about target audience priorities ("who's most important") and arguments ("beyond the numbers, what do we really have to say?").
- Publish a "design brief" that states your understanding of the ground rules; circulate it to the masters and secure their amendments or approval.

- Repeat this step as often as needed. A design brief endorsed by all interested parties will save time and money, reduce angst and do wonders for your disposition.

- Designate — or hire — one bulldog to manage the project. This person plays the same role that a producer does in Hollywood. That is, she/he controls the schedule and budget.

  This person should not — repeat, not — be an employee of the design firm you've chosen to create and produce your report. He/she must be objective… and merciless.

  (*Get rich now and forever scheme:* If you have the skills and temperament, hang out your shingle as an annual report producer, and you'll always have profitable work. You'll get rich simply by keeping a tenth of what you save your clients.)

- Designate a managing editor. He/she should know from experience how to energize and re-energize designers, photographers, illustrators and writers in the face of unreasonable, implacable "requests" from lawyers, investor relations directors, division managers and CFOs.

  Best case, this person is on your staff. But nowhere is it written that you can't go outside if you have to. If you do, look for someone who has been (or is now) a magazine or newspaper editor, someone with savvy and moxie, whose velvet gloves hide iron fists.

  Your managing editor controls content, subject to the producer's time and money edicts.

- Get your designer on board early. This person — as opposed to "this firm" — will be the team's critical player later, so it's important to involve her/him quickly and completely.

  Given the need for "total immersion," I suggest you try hard to find a designer in your neighborhood. Proximity breeds flexibility. New York or Los Angeles "names" might impress bosses, but their locations and schedules can cause horrific problems.

  A year ago, I was part of an annual report team for a southwestern company whose designer lived and worked in the Midwest, 1,000 miles distant. We relied on phones, faxes and FedEx and hoped we wouldn't fall victim to Murphy's Law.

  Naturally, we did. The day we were to present the final mock-up to the CEO, FedEx lost the packet that contained it.

- Hold team meetings often and encourage letting off steam. You're all in a crucible; the pressure builds and all who try to "grin and bear it" are bound to suffer, as will the quality of the annual.

  You may want to have some of these get-togethers "off campus," perhaps over a meal, and to include spouses and significant others. Their understanding and support can make a big difference.

The other

Like annual report assignments, naming projects usually begin in a hyper-orderly way, probably because the people involved know what's ahead and are trying desperately to deny it.

You may be naming a new product or service, a new process or technology, a new company, or you may be renaming an old product, service, process or company. No matter. Fasten your seat belt. You're in for a wild and crazy ride.

(A client of ours, a company that had been around for 125 years, tried, over our objections, to get out from under a deluge of negative publicity by changing its name. Guess what? It not only didn't work, it dug them in deeper. They ended up in bankruptcy court.)

You start by setting criteria, and maybe by cooking up a scorecard like we did for Nuco. Then thesauruses come out. And people start making lists, and the lists get longer and longer and longer and longer. And mundaner and mundaner. At this point, you may turn in frustration to experts, retaining a firm that specializes in this arcane realm.

If so, your expert will probably bring in a "proprietary" computer program, and before you know it, you'll have many, many more names to add to your list. (When two computer companies merged a few years back, the list of candidate names numbered 33,000 by the time some merciful soul called a halt to the death march.)

The lists typically grow until the calendar intervenes. "Oops! We have to introduce X100 in two months. It's time to pick a name. Let's see what we got." Or, "We want to unveil our new corporate name and logo at the annual meeting in 90 days. Let's see what we got."

All this costs money, of course. *The New York Times* recently reported that companies paid naming consultants $100,000 per project, on average, and typically got 700 candidate names for their money.

This to come up with bell ringers such as Oryx, Unum, Unisys and Praxis. Is it worth it? You decide.

Now, let's say you can't get out of a naming project. What can you do to lessen the craziness? I offer you these suggestions, along with my sympathies:

- Make sure all interested parties understand that you are in effect naming a baby; that is, you're engaged in an utterly subjective exercise that's about as likely to achieve unanimity as the U.S. House of Representatives is.

  No one deserves to feel proud if her/his candidate is adopted, or dismayed if it isn't.

- Remind all interested parties that some, if not most, of the great naming successes were greeted with derision and disagreement when they were introduced. "An oil company named after a sea shell?"

  (Speaking of oil companies, several directors of the Standard Oil Co. of New York were reputedly stupefied when the staff proposed an adjective to replace SOCONY. "Mobil? You gotta be kidding!")

This suggests that great names are sometimes hard to spot. Rarely are they accompanied by an epiphany, a "Eureka!," a "That's it!"

- Remind all interested parties that chances are very good that the name you all finally choose won't be available. The fact that so many English words and word combinations have already been copyrighted (often preemptively) explains why you see names like Oryx and Unum.

- Restore their fallen spirits by making it clear that the name itself is far less important than what you do with it.

   (To stay on the oil company track for the moment, there weren't many huzzahs when Standard Oil of New Jersey became Exxon, but the name has worked well for the company over the years.)

- Make sure your teammates understand that the proper starting point for a naming project is a precise definition of what it is you're naming. If you're naming a product or service, start by spelling out its benefits and attributes. If you're naming a company, start by detailing who it is, what it stands for, where it wants to go, its character, culture and personality, its competitors. Use the planning blueprint described in chapter one of this book.

   Pardon the pun, but a name is nothing more than a communications strategy by another name. Successful names stand on carefully constructed foundations.

- Make sure you have an all-star designer on your team from the get-go. The visual is at least as important as the verbal.

- Work with your designer to create prototypes that show how candidate names would actually be used. Seeing your favorites on the sides of trucks and water towers or at the bottom of ads will either reinforce your opinion or cause you to change it.

- While it's true that miracles happen, that someone may indeed come up with a "10" (e.g., Common Cause), they don't happen often, so be prepared to settle for an "8.5" — secure in the knowledge that intelligent, consistent implementation will turn it into a "9.5."

- Remember, you're naming something that you hope will be around for a long time, so a name that wears well is more important than a name that makes a good first impression.

   In fact, the best names often don't make good first impressions because they're different, unexpected. They're like a new pair of really good shoes. You have to wear them for awhile before they're comfortable, but once they are, they stay that way for a long, long time.

- Gain agreement from all interested parties on the type of name you're looking for. The choices? Here's a menu:
   - *Eponymous.* Names that borrow from people, usually real (Ford, Hewlett-Packard), but not always (Sara Lee)
   - *Descriptive.* Names that describe activities, attitudes and/or markets (International Business Machines, Elite Cleaners, Farmers Insurance)

How does your logo sound?

When we create product, service or corporate identities, we strive for a look that's distinctive, attractive and appropriate — as well we should. There's another dimension, however, that's also worth thinking about. Let's call it "aural equivalence."

Given that your logo will almost certainly "appear" on media that offer sound in addition to, or instead of, sight, it's important to build into it a distinctive, attractive, appropriate sound, too. Think NBC. Their bong-bong-bong is as identifiable as their peacock.

- *Suggestive.* Names that hint at activities, attitudes and/or markets (Technicolor, Polaroid, the Foresight Institute, Steelcase, Vise Grip)
- *Acronyms.* Pronounceable names derived from other words (Arco, Alcoa, Texaco, the Rand Institute, with "rand" cleverly standing in for "research and development")
- *Initials.* Combinations of letters that aren't pronounceable, so the letters must be spoken individually, also known as alphabet soup (RCA, CBS, AT&T)
- *Analogous.* Names that borrow words from other realms to make a point (Quaker Oats, Best Foods, Chevron, Pampers, Caterpillar)
- *Abstractions.* Names that build particular meanings into appealing words (Arrow, Apple, Camel)
- *Coined.* Names that build particular meanings into made-up words (Kodak, Exxon, Acura, Motorola)
- *Geographic.* Names that tie to places (Texas Instruments, Boston Consulting Group, Kentucky Fried Chicken — a name recently changed to KFC, presumably because those in charge felt "Kentucky" was either limiting or had lost the positive connotation it had once been thought to have)
- *Combinations of the above.* Like Mrs. Field's Cookies, Boston Scientific and Allegheny Ludlum

• Remind your team to consider the "forgettability factor" as they review these alternatives; that is, some name types are harder (i.e., more expensive) to implant on your target audiences than others.

For example, initials and acronyms, those favorites of governments everywhere, are much harder for people to remember than eponymous and analogous names, so if you don't have a lot of time and money to invest to establish your name with your target audiences, don't call yourself ZXO or QAPO.

We all tend to forget that the names we remember are those we've been exposed to time and again (Nike, Levi's, Microsoft)...and that somebody's paying for all that exposure (hundreds of millions of dollars per year in the case of the three examples).

Turning a name into an identity or a brand franchise is a very, very expensive proposition. How deep are your pockets?

- Agree on scoring criteria. Here are mine:
  - distinctive
  - memorable
  - tolerable (a.k.a. wears well)
  - accurate
  - believable
  - easy to speak/pronounce on the phone
  - easy to understand when heard
  - visually and verbally appealing
  - states or implies a positive distinguishing feature or benefit
  - is properly understood by all target audiences in all current and potential marketplaces
  - is available and protectable

Regarding the penultimate criterion, I'm sure you've heard some of the blunders made by companies that don't check out what their upstanding English names and graphics mean in other languages and cultures. Chevrolet's Nova, for example, carried a name that means "doesn't go" in Spanish.

Here are a few other examples:

- An airline lost passengers when it touted its "rendezvous lounges" in Brazil. It seems "rendezvous" in Portugese is a place to have sex.
- McDonald's ran into trouble when it promoted "Big Macs" in French-speaking Quebec where the term is slang for large breasts.
- A toothpaste's promise of "white teeth" didn't cut it in parts of Southeast Asia where gray teeth (from chewing betel nuts) are a status symbol.
- A brand of baby food whose labels showed smiling infants caused consternation among some in Africa who deduced from the label that the jars contained ground-up babies.

Tales like these are less amusing when you're the poor soul whose team was responsible for the inapt strategy; so if you plan to publish your work internationally, be careful. Have it checked by people who are familiar with both the languages and cultures of all the places it will appear.

Incidentally, the Internet provides a quick and easy way to do this, at least provisionally. Post your work online and invite reactions.

A matter of interpretation

In the 1950s, the U.S. State Department showed incoming Foreign Service Officers a training film on how to use an interpreter that featured an American diplomat speaking through a Vietnamese interpreter to a village elder. One evening, a public television program showed a clip from this film, and a college professor who spoke Vietnamese happened to be watching.

He called the State Department immediately to advise them that the training film inadvertently made quite a different, and more important, point. It showed what can happen when no one involved in the film's production pays attention to content.

That's right. The Vietnamese interpreter was taking liberties. The diplomat would say, "Your rice crop looks good," and his interpreter would translate, "Your breath is bad this morning." Or words to this effect.

When I was shown this film as a new recruit, my trainers advertised it as having a dual purpose: to show us how to use an interpreter, and to show us what happens when you don't pay attention to the interpretations.

Don't let what happened to the State Department happen to you. Double check all translations. When you have something translated from English into Vietnamese, say, take the translation you get from interpreter A to interpreter B, and ask B to translate it back to English.

Chapter 19

No Guts, No Glory

"I want my mommy."

It had been a tough afternoon on the Commons floor, and the PM was in a foul mood. What was worse, he now had to sit for a portrait photograph. "Be quick about it," he muttered to the young photographer as he sat in the designated chair.

"Would you mind taking the cigar out of your mouth?" asked the photographer.

"Yes, as a matter of fact, I would," growled the PM.

Whereupon the photographer marched up to his subject, removed the cigar, raced back to his camera and snapped the famous photo of a brooding, scowling Winston Churchill.

Incidentally, the portrait also made the artist quite famous. His name: Yousuf Karsh. He was 22 years old when he made his bold, disarming move, and he went on to become of the two or three most popular portrait photographers of our time.

Disarming. That was the key to his great success, I reckon. Karsh had the courage to do something shockingly unexpected. He so surprised his subject that, for a second — long enough to record it — the great man's mask fell away.

And the photographer achieved what every communications strategist aims for: a breakthrough.

Unmasking a president

Speaking of masks falling away, I once wrote and produced a film that aimed to persuade young people to vote and featured former presidents Gerald Ford and Jimmy Carter being interviewed by a young actress playing the role of college newspaper reporter.

I'd let both men know ahead of time what sorts of questions to expect, but I'd also had myself "wired" to the actress so I could feed her additional questions if they occurred to me. Exactly this happened as she and Carter were strolling down the main (and only) street of Plains, Ga.

I thought of a question that not only wasn't in my briefing memo, it was maybe too personal and borderline provocative. What to do? Have the actress ask it and risk disrupting the interview, interrupt the interview myself and check it out with Carter (which would deprive it of its zing), or drop it altogether? I decided to take a chance, toss a curve ball, and I had her put this question to Carter:

"Mr. President, what would you say if your daughter Amy (who was 21 or 22 at the time) told you she wasn't going to vote?"

In a millisecond, the former president stepped down from his presidential pedestal and became a loving, caring, passionate father. He got this hell's fire look in his eye and stammered, "Why…I…I think…I'd disown her."

Needless to say, his spontaneous expression of an unvarnished truth became our film's lead (with his enthusiastic approval), as well as the opening segment of a television commercial we created to promote a network documentary on voting.

Goodbye, data

The point of these anecdotes is, of course, that there inevitably comes a time when communications strategists and their colleagues and sponsors have to walk away from all their data, heed their intuitions and take a chance…or forever hold their peace.

I don't care how much time and money you invest in what kinds of research. You'll never know all you want to. In some respects, research data are like money (you never have enough), and in other respects, they're even more provocative (they raise questions at the same time they provide answers).

It surely makes good sense to use research, but it makes no sense to rely exclusively on it. Research is properly a guide, not a crutch. Given that communication, finally, is an art form, all research can do is to lay the groundwork and strengthen the foundation upon which the art stands, the cornerstones.

If your communications are to get heard, they have to possess a quality research can't give them. They have to make an emotional connection, trigger reflexive wows, smiles, double takes and sympathetic vibrations. (My free association here: Cinderella's fairy godmother using her magic wand to "inspire" your speeches, presentations, brochures, videos and ad campaigns.)

So nerve up. You have nothing to lose but your job. And if you position your roll of the dice properly, it might strengthen your hold on your job. Bosses tend to admire risk takers, if only because that's probably what enabled them to become bosses.

Data dismissed

Sometimes rolling the dice means going with your instincts absent supporting data, and sometimes it means trusting them in the face of data that point in another direction. The then CEO of Avis had to turn his back on a persuasive body of evidence when he OK'd "We're number 2; we try harder." His research people plied him with charts and graphs that "proved" the folly of claiming second place.

He also trusted his advertising guru, who told him with obvious conviction and great passion that the campaign would work, who had the guts to bet the Avis account on his people's artistry. "You can feel the theme's power," he said. "It plays to Americans' inclination to root for the underdog."

By the way, "playing to Americans' inclination to root for the underdog" is a good example of a campaign idea, also known as a communications strategy.

Its implementation in the face of research that said "don't" also provides a compelling contrast to Coca-Cola's exhaustively researched misadventure into "New Coke."

Sometimes you lose

Business journalists were having a field day. A venerable blue chip had "stumbled" thanks to a couple of "harebrained" decisions by its new chief executive. We were asked to help the company repair its tarnished image.

When we did our homework, we learned three things: First, the decisions weren't "harebrained." Quite the opposite. When you understood the reasons for them, they made a lot of sense.

Second, the company's "stumbles" had, in fact, placed it squarely on a path to become a stronger and more resilient competitor.

Third, no one in the target audience (investors, customers, regulators, employees) was inclined to listen to — or believe — anything the company or its CEO said.

The company's communications people had mishandled the situation from day one — stonewalling, denying, fudging, overpromising — often in the name of the new CEO. In the process, they had created a serious credibility problem and exacerbated an already serious misperception problem.

Lemonade, anyone?

So what's a communications strategist to do? You work with what you got, right? And what we had, what we thought we had, was an opportunity to turn a lemon into lemonade. At the appointed hour, in the company's pine-paneled boardroom on a Saturday afternoon, we unveiled our strategy to the chief executive and his direct reports.

As we presented our work, our audience grew visibly and audibly enthusiastic — huzzahs all around — with one exception. The boss sat poker-faced, puffing on his Don Diego Lonsdale.

This was disconcerting, to say the least, because, as you've probably guessed, he was the star of the strategy. Borrowing an idea from the Japanese martial arts, we proposed to use the force of the attacks on him to help repel them.

We reckoned that the best way to re-engage a target audience that had closed its eyes, ears and minds was to acknowledge their views. Humorously. With tongue gently in cheek. By having a little fun with the boss — and with his unusual first name, the press having seized on it derisively in its reports.

Wherefore art thou, Edgar?

So, for example, we created an ad that showed a large illustrated eight ball, with a character in the foreground peering around it and asking, "You back there, Edgar?"

The response, "No, I'm over here," was in the form of a stylized word balloon that led readers to the body copy, which put the "stumbles" in the proper context.

Another ad showed the same character staring into a prominent black hole and asking, "You down there, Edgar?" followed by the same response.

Perhaps our most unconventional proposal concerned a critical refinancing plan that the company had just negotiated with 225 banks. We recommended running a full-page ad in the *Wall Street Journal* the day the deal was done with a one-word headline in small type floating in a sea of white space. The word: "Whew."

Our plan was comprehensive. We'd prepared a video storyboard that featured Edgar (not his real name) poking fun at himself as he and others told the company's story. We'd even created posters and mailers that had fun with Edgar's well-known love of cigars (e.g., a caricature of a half-smoked stogie captioned, "No, the chairman does not roll his own").

The roar of the crowd

Our audience that Saturday afternoon roared its approval, and our spirits were correspondingly high. Not for long, though. Two days later, the company's communications vice president told us that the CEO had told her, "If we run those ads, I'll be a laughingstock."

Two months later, the company launched radio and television ads that featured smiling people singing, "We're not giving up, we're moving on," based on lots of research, no doubt. Two months after that, the company's board of directors fired the CEO.

When your gut says no

Let's turn the coin over. Suppose the Avis CEO had felt uncomfortable with "We're No. 2." What should he have said to his impassioned ad man? Or, suppose his research people had supported it along with his ad man, but he felt uncomfortable nonetheless. What then?

It's tempting to argue that trusting your gut isn't a sometime thing. You either do it, or you don't. But my gut won't buy this view. It seems both logical and simplistic to me. There are nuances to be considered, degrees, intensities.

Is your gut roaring or just whispering? Are you reacting to particular words and pictures, to the idea/strategy that underlies them, or to something else entirely, some other hidden thing? What specifically does your research have to say? Are there other paths to explore before you decide finally ("third ways")? Is there time?

When my gut says no, I try first to buy some time. "I want to sleep on this." Then I use this time to listen to myself. I settle into a quiet place, by myself, and muse. "What's going on here? What's really bothering me about the communication?" Then I seek out those who are in favor of it and listen to them. "Talk to me about why you feel as you do. What's your gut saying to you? How loudly?"

All this listening usually tempers the conflicts I might feel between my head and heart and between my views and others' views, and we're able to reach a salutary resolution. As former President Lyndon Johnson said, "When it comes to making decisions, timing is everything."

However, if after all the listening and all the discussing, my gut still roars, "No!" I heed it, and I suggest you do the same.

Savor your victories

In baseball a .250 hitter is trade bait. A communications strategist who connects a quarter of the time is a candidate for the hall of fame.

There are so many variables, so many players, so many opportunities for Murphy's Law to take effect, that almost "nothing succeeds as planned," to borrow a wonderful line from Joseph Heller's wonderful novel, *Good as Gold*.

So if you're easily discouraged, or disinclined to persevere when the odds against you are long, you should probably consider another line of work.

The flip side, of course, ought to be that the occasional victory tastes especially good. Indeed, that's sometimes true. But not always.

We once presented a full-blown communications initiative that we were particularly proud of because it resolved what the client saw as an impossible issue. Our basic idea was visual, a "framework" that allowed us to tell a variety of stories.

Our client's marketing vice president, the ultimate authority, saw things differently, thought our framework too limiting, and sent us back to the drawing board. "I want options," he said, "and I don't want to wait till I get back to see them." (He was leaving the next day for a three-week trip through the Orient.)

We dutifully came up with five options ("A," "B," "D," "E" and "F"), which we shipped to our fearless leader's Tokyo hotel, along with a minimally tweaked version of our original recommendation ("C"). Four days later, our client's strategic communications vice president got a terse communique from his marketing counterpart: "Go with C."

What happened? Who knows? We weren't about to ask, and neither were those involved on the client side. Maybe it was jet lag, or a delicious dinner, or the weather. We'll never know.

What we do know, however, is that the communications business is a capricious one, where both victories and defeats are often incomprehensible. Your batting average is determined in great part by how you cope with the glitches, how quickly you recover and how successfully you can keep things in perspective.

I've had clients yell, scream, walk out, doze off, throw my work and spit on it, but the ultimate test of my personal commitment to the communications business came out of the blue one day. Two colleagues and I were meeting with three senior executives from our client organization whom I'll call Tom, Dick and Harry. We were discussing routine matters, nothing controversial. At one point, though, after Tom made what seemed to me to be a reasonable comment, Dick, a burly fellow who probably weighed 250 pounds, leapt out of his chair, grabbed him by the lapels on his jacket and threatened to beat him up. Fortunately, Harry was able to cool off the would-be attacker, and no blood was shed. The meeting ended posthaste, and I never did find out what prompted Dick's explosion.

A matter of guts

Picture this: a full-page newspaper ad, two-thirds of which is an illustration of a faceless man being held by two masked terrorists. One holds an Uzi submachine gun at his side. The other is pointing a .45-caliber pistol at the faceless captive's temple.

Headline: If terrorists held you captive, how much press coverage would you want?

When Jeff, the client company's executive vice president for public affairs, and I presented this ad in layout form to the company's president and chairman, both blanched ("Do we have to?") but neither rejected it explicitly.

I decided I'd do Jeff a favor and tone down the illustration. I had an overlay drawn that moved the pistol from the captive's temple to the terrorist's hip. But when I showed it to Jeff, his reaction wasn't gratitude. It was indignation. "That's a compromise," he said, "and we can't afford compromises. Run the ad with the pistol where it belongs."

The day the ad ran (in a dozen papers in major markets around the country), the company's president steamed into Jeff's office. "I never said you could run this ad," he bellowed. "But you never said we couldn't," Jeff replied. "And advertising's my responsibility, and I thought it was a great ad."

The president nodded, turned on his heel and returned to his office. The ad pulled a record number of requests for information…and no complaints.

On another occasion, our art director came up with a great idea for a campaign we were working on for Jeff's company. She wanted to commission a brilliant but controversial European artist to illustrate the ads.

We sounded out Jeff. He liked the notion. I called the artist who said, "I'd like to do it. It will be a first for me. No company has ever used me before. I guess I'm too controversial."

I asked how much time he needed and how much he'd charge. "You send me your sketches and $7,500, and 72 hours later, I'll send you the first piece of finished art."

"What if we don't like it?" I asked.

"Send me another $7,500," he replied, "and I'll do it over."

I figured that was that. A controversial artist who'd never done sponsored work before and wanted the king's ransom? Never happen. But when I told Jeff what I'd learned, he surprised me again.

"It's only money," Jeff said. "Send him the $7,500."

Jeff was right again, of course. We got masterpieces for our money and a spectacular multimedia campaign.

Moral: After all the planning, all the research, all the evaluation procedures and all the meetings, if you want really great communications, you have to be prepared to trust your gut and roll the dice.

Chapter 20

Last Gasps

"And in closing, my friends…"

Now that you appreciate that:

- "getting heard" is a competitive endeavor of Olympian proportions;
- well-developed strategies are as essential to "getting heard" as they are to winning gold medals, government contracts or chess matches, and
- the blueprint outlined in the previous chapters provides a methodology to develop winning strategies,

I can add a few tips, tricks and pitfall-avoidance procedures to the blueprint's margins.

The Fire Swamp

If you read William Goldman's wonderful novel, *The Princess Bride*, or saw Rob Reiner's almost-as-wonderful film adaptation of it, you'll recall that the princess bride and her true love are forced into the dread Fire Swamp to escape the bad guys.

As they make their way through this thoroughly inhospitable place, they — and the readers and viewers who follow them — are subjected to a series of surprise attacks, perpetrated by grotesque and netherworldly creatures.

It's Goldman at his most imaginative. You're smiling and biting your nails at the same time; on the edge of your easy chair or theater seat waiting for the next unpleasantness. You know it will come, but not where it will come from or what shape it will take.

Following the blueprint to *Getting Heard* is not unlike wading through the Fire Swamp. On the one hand, it's an easy-to-understand route with markers, milestones and checkpoints. But to follow the path it lays out is to subject yourself to a series of surprise attacks.

You know they're coming. You don't know when, where or from whom.

Sometimes, though, they tip their hand, telegraph their punch, give you warning… if you know the code. Here's what to listen for:

"Chris, your blueprint makes sense in theory, but this is the real world. Our new widgets will be ready to ship in six weeks and we have to get the word out."

Run this through the Captain Marvel decoder implant between your ears and this is what comes out: "I don't buy your view that `getting heard' is hard. The people we want to talk to hear us just fine."

"Chris, your blueprint is elegant and absolutely necessary…if we were remodeling our offices or retooling our production line. But we're not. We're just talking to our friends. We should invest the money where we know it will do us some good."

When your Marvel decoder unscrambles this one, it comes out: "I only bet on sure things, unless I'm desperate. And I'm not desperate."

"Chris, the approach you propose with this blueprint of yours is really interesting, really, really interesting."

Decode the message here and you get, "I'm on the fence, and I'm gonna stay there."

There are endless variations, of course, but these three themes cover almost all bushwhacking offensives (a.k.a. ambushes). So how do you deal with them?

Wading through

The first step is to let your attacker know that you've decoded the message.

Step two is to send a few coded messages of your own that play to your attacker's fears, hopes and frustrations. You can cite independent studies, for instance, that illustrate how difficult it is to get heard nowadays.

"Jan, our target audience will be exposed to 300 sales pitches the day ours arrives and they may remember three. The odds against us are 100 to one."

Or, you can turn it around. "Jan, how many messages do you guess the people we want to buy our 50,000 widgets will be exposed to on the day we deliver ours? How many do you guess they'll remember?"

Or, "Jan, if your life were on the line, if you were about to do battle with an enemy that outnumbered you 100 to one, wouldn't you want to prepare yourself in every possible way?"

You can ask Jan the questions I asked you at the beginning of this book. "How many of the communications you were exposed to yesterday do you remember today? How many did you pay attention to? How many did you act on?"

You can position your initiative as equivalent to taking out a life insurance policy before you set out on a trek to the Himalayas. "There's a lot at stake here, Jan, including our jobs, and the mountain we have to climb is a monster. We have 90 days to persuade 50,000 people to kick a habit — to stop buying our rivals' widgets and start buying ours. Let's make sure we're prepared."

(You may want to get a little more personal, remind your adversaries that they have mortgages, orthodontists' bills and kids who deserve the same quality of education they received. Or recall how long it took former colleagues to find jobs after they lost theirs. Scare the bejeezus out of them, in other words.)

You can talk dollars and sense. "Jan, we aim to sell 50,000 widgets for $100 each. We're going to invest $500,000 in marketing communications to make this happen. Suppose they miss the mark. What are the consequences? Maybe we only sell 40,000 widgets, and we lose a million bucks, plus the half million we spent on our communications. Now, what's it worth to make sure we don't lose a million and a half dollars?"

You can take the high road, appeal to their professional pride and self-respect, focus on the payoffs. "Jan, this is our chance to do something really well, to be the professionals that we are, to show our colleagues and superiors what happens when you really pay attention, discipline yourself and plan like the big folks do. Imagine their reaction when we don't sell 50,000 widgets — we sell 60,000. How will we ever be able to look at ourselves in a mirror again if we don't take it?"

When you're up to your neck

Step three is to negotiate. Follow the blueprint, but reduce its dimensions and fast-track it. Two friendly words of warning: Whatever you do, don't give up the methodology — the alternative is adhocracy, a surefire failure — and make sure you scale back your objective along with everything else.

By the shores of old Lake Bullbleep

The vocabulary of a business tells you something about it, and the vocabulary of the communications business is no exception. "Songs and dances," "smoke and mirrors," "image polishing," "finessing," "spin control," these words and phrases suggest a discomfiting truth: We communications people have traditionally been paid to "put the best face on things," to "put our best foot forward" — to use our sleight-of-hand

194

skills to shift our target audiences' attention away from flaws and blotches to the "good things we're doing."

This tradition is dying, thank goodness, laid low by its own excesses and by the microchip. All of us, including our target audiences, now have so much information from so many sources at our fingertips that some of it is almost sure to expose attempts at what I call "truth tempering."

And, of course, with every exposure, we all become a little more cynical, a little more wary and a lot less inclined to believe anything. And why not? Things rarely are as they seem. A respected industrialist and arts patron turns out to have been probably a Soviet agent. Thanks to the First Amendment and enterprising journalists, we regularly discover that some respected public official is on the take. A *Reader's Digest* ad aimed at marketing people said it all: "The four toughest words you face today: 'I don't believe you.'"

The question then becomes, how do we get people who are predisposed not to believe us to change the way they feel? One good answer is to cop to our hallowed truth-tempering habits and kick them. We have to begin by changing our views of ourselves and our professional roles.

No more babies, puppies and cheesecake?

This means convincing ourselves that the old tricks no longer work like they used to; that babies, puppies, blondes atop fenders, back-yard barbecues in OzzieandHarrietville, and skinny, smiley actors and actresses are losing their powers of persuasion.

It means convincing ourselves that we aren't the clowns who follow the elephants with oversized brooms and dustpans; that our job is not to add gloss, hide missteps and generally distract people's attention from the messes. No, our job is to explicate the messes and put them in context.

A diplomat I know puts it well: "It's no longer what truths to tell. Now it's how to tell the truth."

When I first started writing ad copy, there was an adage that was popular with both colleagues and clients: "The masses are asses." I didn't believe it then, and I don't believe it now. The masses are far smarter than the writers who condescend to them, if only because they've had so many slippery sales pitches tossed at them.

If I could impart only one thing to help you make your communications more effective, it would be this: The masses aren't asses. If you want them to hear and believe you, be respectful, be real and talk straight.

It's so simple and yet so hard. Tell them the truth. Just tell them the truth.

Being

We live in a noisy, hype-filled era when the adage "Talk is cheap" is more widely believed than ever. We're all skeptics. So it is that to claim something without supporting evidence is to invite your target audience to disbelieve it. ("I am not a crook.")

A communications strategist's responses to this state of affairs are (1) to create messages that convey demonstrations of the argument; (2) to create messages that are themselves demonstrations of the argument; or (3) to create messages that are both.

For example, let's say Red Inc. wants to communicate its innovativeness (its name gives it a head start, eh?). Best case, Red's communications will be innovative. They will prompt Red's target audiences to do a double take when they see them. "Wow!," their inner voices will whisper. "That's neat."

And they will prompt Red's target audiences to say to one another, "That Red's a pretty sharp outfit," and to write letters, articles, speeches and "60 Minutes" scripts that salute Red's ability to "think outside the dots."

(It will, of course, help Red's communications strategists if Red's offering is, in fact, a consequence of thinking outside the dots; if, as Henry Kissinger used to say, "It has the added benefit of being true.")

Now, what will Red's communications not do? They will not use the adjective "innovative." Unless, of course, Red's communications strategists come up with a genuinely innovative way to do so.

In a world of pretending, authenticity stands out.

You don't know what you don't know

When you shift your focus from finessing to explicating, an interesting thing happens. You discover that your target audiences don't always know what they want to hear. In fact, they *often* don't know what they want to hear. And this leads you to ask yourself, "What do we know that our target audiences would probably think was helpful if they knew it?"

To pose this question is to open a whole bunch of windows — and to prompt return visits and deeper conversations with product designers, engineers, manufacturing types and systems integrators. "Why did you put this gizmo here? What were you thinking? What facts, feelings, hunches or intuitions prompted it?"

Let's say your assignment is to put together a communications initiative in the United States, Canada and Mexico for the British Tourist Board that aims to attract first-time visitors to London. If you ask your target audience what would cause them to consider visiting London, they'll feed back what they know about London from books, films, newspapers, magazines. "Buckingham Palace," "The Tower of London," "Big Ben," "Parliament," "The Thames," "Westminster Abbey."

But, in fact, what they might appreciate more than a brochure that gurgled about all these worthy attractions is a map of London's streets and Underground. They just don't know to ask for it because, never having visited London, never having tried to get from Chelsea to Piccadilly, they wouldn't know how tricky it is to navigate Great Britain's "Great City."

As outlandish and heretical as it may seem, it's coming to pass that even advertising, that quintessential image-burnishing tool, is focusing now and then on presenting information that target audiences would find useful if they knew to ask for it. The goal is still persuasion, of course, but the strategy has changed. Now, the best sell is no sell; it's to present useful information in an unvarnished way.

Is this an aberration or the beginning of a sea change? Time will tell. Meanwhile, a pair of college professors who study the subject have written an article that predicts that the advertising industry will be transformed, that ads will help consumers acquire individualized information and will perhaps even charge for the service they provide. Stranger things have happened, but not much stranger. Can you imagine a time when audiences will come to regard ads as valuable resources rather than mostly banal intrusions on their lives?

In fact, if we temper this picture a bit, the time is now. There are ads today that are valuable resources. I cut them out. You probably do, too. But pay for them? I don't know.

Whither slogans?

Will there be room for slogans in this brave new world? Or are slogans, by definition, image-burnishers? Yes and no. Yes, there will be ample room for slogans that express an organization's character or legitimate aspirations or credibly promise a real benefit to their target audiences.

No, there won't be room for slogans that make unsupported claims or describe their sponsors' activities or attitudes in "boilerplatese."

Here are examples of both kinds. Can you tie them to their sponsors? Which ones would you put into the "useful in our time" category?

Slogan	Sponsor
A more productive way of working.	American Airlines
A tradition of trust.	Archer Daniels Midland
Be all you can be.	Buick
Creating a higher standard.	Cadillac
In touch with tomorrow.	Electronic Data Systems
Just do it.	Ford
Live free or die.	General Electric
Our strengths are legendary.	IBM
Quality is job #1.	Lexus
Semper fi.	Lincoln
Solutions for a small planet.	Merrill Lynch
Something special in the air.	Motorola
Supermarket to the world.	New Hampshire
The document company.	Nike
The new symbol for quality in America.	Samsonite
The world's most refreshing airline.	Swissair

The relentless pursuit of perfection.   Toshiba

We bring good things to life.   U.S. Army

What a luxury car should be.   U.S. Marine Corps

What you never thought possible.   Xerox

Here are the correct match-ups:

Sponsor	Slogan
American Airlines	Something special in the air.
Archer Daniels Midland	Supermarket to the world.
Buick	The new symbol for quality in America.
Cadillac	Creating a higher standard.
Electronic Data Systems	A more productive way of working.
Ford	Quality is job #1.
General Electric	We bring good things to life.
IBM	Solutions for a small planet.
Lexus	The relentless pursuit of perfection.
Lincoln	What a luxury car should be.
Merrill Lynch	A tradition of trust.
Motorola	What you never thought possible.
New Hampshire	Live free or die.
Nike	Just do it.
Samsonite	Our strengths are legendary.
Swissair	The world's most refreshing airline.
Toshiba	In touch with tomorrow.
U.S. Army	Be all you can be.
U.S. Marine Corps	Semper fi.
Xerox	The document company.

How did you do?

For the record, my candidates for the "useful in our time" category are: Archer Daniels Midland's "Supermarket to the world," Ford's "Quality is job #1," IBM's "Solutions for a small planet," New Hampshire's "Live free or die," Nike's "Just do it," Samsonite's "Our strengths are legendary," the U.S. Army's "Be all you can be," the U.S. Marine Corps' "Semper fi" and Xerox's "The document company."

I chose these because they are memorably, beneficially descriptive (e.g., Archer Daniels Midland), because they make a valuable, credible promise (e.g., the U.S. Army), or because they are inspirational and energizing (e.g., New Hampshire).

If you were to ask me to help you come up with a slogan for your outfit, I would first ask you why you thought a slogan would help you achieve your goals. Second, I would make sure you understood why slogans are often a bad idea (forgettable, conventional boilerplate, expensive to get across to target audiences). And third, I would probably urge you to think in terms of a rallying cry ("Just do it") rather than something descriptive ("The document company").

The difference between rallying cries and descriptive slogans is the difference between elevator music and the Rolling Stones.

Rallying cries are not only more memorable, they're also motivational. At least, the good ones are.

(For the record, my own company, Yonder, sports a rallying cry: "Off we go.")

The Churchill implication

No, that's not Robert Ludlum's latest potboiler novel. It's a way to talk about how some communications strategists use market research.

According to one of Winston Churchill's biographers, the great man saw political polls as instruments to measure how successful he was in communicating *his* ideas. He aimed to shape public opinion rather than play to it, and polls helped him judge how well he was doing.

Some communications strategists see a similar role for their polls. They're putting their carts ahead of their horses, so to speak (leading the elephants!), determining their arguments first, then using market research to measure how well they did.

I don't make the rules...

I once created a television commercial for Stars and Stripes cupcakes in which the announcer was supposed to say, to Souza's march music, "Stars and Stripes, for lunch, for dinner, for snacks, forever." But when the storyboard arrived on the network censors' desks, one rejected it, arguing that the line encouraged young people to overeat.

So I returned to the drawing board and rewrote the line as follows: "Stars and Stripes, for lunch, for dinner, for snacks, for fun." And, guess what, the same censor OKed it.

I mention this because communications strategists should be aware that, the First Amendment notwithstanding, there are armies of private and public-sector regulators who matter. They are, in effect, an "over the shoulder" target audience. And their orientation is that the sponsor is considered guilty until it proves otherwise.

They also tend to be humorless. Years ago, a television advertiser storyboarded a spot that featured comedian Redd Foxx saying, "Marshmallows make your eyes turn blue." It was rejected because it was determined (note the passive voice) that some in the audience might not get the joke and would therefore be deceived.

Finally, regulators tend to be unsympathetic to the argument that, since the purpose of marketing communications is persuasion, they need only tell those truths that are persuasive, so long as they don't mislead. Regulators typically want to see all the facts, relevant and irrelevant. That's why there are so many unreadable footnotes and superimpositions crammed into modern ads, brochures, TV spots, et. al.

The point: Be prepared, define this target audience, too, and invent your communications strategies with them in mind.

The computer did it!

The client had taken a booth at an upcoming convention in Dallas and needed a capabilities brochure to pass out. There was only one problem: The convention began in 10 days. Faced with this unpleasant fact, we decided to work with a designer who could do the whole job on a computer — art, copy, design, mechanical assembly, film, the works.

He finished his layout on Friday evening and faxed hard copies to three client executives at their homes and to me. We called our changes in to him on Saturday. He faxed revised hard copy. We called in more changes. He faxed revised, revised hard copy. By Sunday afternoon, everyone was satisfied, and he was given the go-ahead to have the piece printed.

Five days later, 500 copies were shipped to the client's Dallas hotel and as soon as he received them, he called to say how much he liked them and how grateful he was that we were able to meet his difficult deadline. A tough job well done.

Not quite. The day after the convention ended, he called me again. It seems there was a little problem with the brochure. We'd misspelled the CEO's name on the cover.

How could such a thing happen? I checked the hard copy the designer had sent me, and the name was spelled correctly (Whew!) I called the designer, who pulled the job up on his computer screen and discovered it was spelled incorrectly. Huh?

Turns out he had faxed us oversized pages to make it easier for us to read the copy; then, once everything had been approved, he'd reduced them to ready them for printing and, somehow, his computer had excised a letter when it made the reductions.

Not just any letter, mind you. A letter from the boss' name. Naturally. Which highlights anew something we all know all too well: There are gremlins in your computer and, if you're not careful, they'll eat you alive.

Can you spot the mistakes?

An excerpt from a preeminent consulting company's annual report:

> *"The project's success has lead to Blank Consulting being engaged by various departments of Blank Client for assistance on other projects."*

Incidentally, the authors of this report also described success as "epehemeral" (how appropriate is that?) and located one of the firm's offices in "Basal, Switzerland."

Headline on an insurance company ad that ran in a news magazine's special section on education and the arts:

> *"A capacity and taste for reading gives access to whatever has already been discovered by others..." A. Lincoln*

The interesting question here is who boobooed — Abe, some other Lincoln whose first name begins with "A" or the copywriter who stole the quote?

The ninth wave

I mentioned Eugene Burdick's wonderful novel in chapter nine. Now I'd like to bring it back. You may recall that *The Ninth Wave* tells the story, metaphorically, of a surfer who sets out at dawn in search of the perfect wave and returns at sunset without having ridden any. He lets every wave go by because he thinks the one behind it may be the perfect ("ninth") wave.

Communications being as subjective, visible and hard-to-measure as they are, they sometimes have a similarly paralyzing effect on organizations. They get tongue-tied, opting to stay silent until the perfect communications program presents itself.

The people responsible are inclined to say, "Yes, this brochure makes the points I want to make, but how do I know how many of my prospects will read it and be persuaded by it? Maybe another approach would attract more of them. Do you have alternatives?"

Now, given that any competent writer/art director/designer team can come up with alternatives *ad nauseam*, here we have a prescription for paralysis. Please note: Given a set of variables, engineers and financial types seek *the* answer — the one right answer, while communications types seek the best of an infinite number of "right answers," given the time and money available. (The associative process is open-ended.) This dichotomy can produce serious, anger-making, paralyzing misunderstandings.

There are two ways out of the box. First, point out that silence carries a price tag just as surely as communicating does. No one has ever managed to sell an unknown, invisible product, service or point of view. A "low profile" is sometimes called for. A "no profile" rarely is.

Second, experiment. Test programs in particular markets, learn from them and modify them as results warrant. Communications are organic. They're meant to grow and change and improve and teach. The more you do it, the better you get at it. Just like golf, writing and almost everything else.

Perhaps the best thing about the methodology I've presented in this book is that it produces information that makes the next iteration better, by definition.

In the course of implementing your strategies, you and your colleagues will see how your target audiences react to them, and these reactions will cause you to revisit your situation analysis, which will cause you to redefine your cornerstones, which will prompt you to invent new strategies…and so it goes, continuous improvement.

Onward and upward. Good luck!

Dos and don'ts

Do

Say it with feeling. Communications that prompt an emotional response from your target audience are much more powerful than those that don't.

Be interesting. Focus on your target audience's concerns, be instructive and succinct. Remember, though, that communications that make you laugh, smile or relax at the end of a long day are instructive.

Be indirect. Don't tell your target audience that your widget is great. Give them reasons for its greatness, and leave it at that.

Understate. When everyone else is yelling, a whisper stands out.

Be careful with humor. It's powerful if well done. Just make sure it's funny, really funny, to your target audience.

Feature people. We're all interested in the lives of others. Curiosity is genetic.

Remember, almost right is wrong. Better to be quiet and save your money.

Remember, euphemisms are wet blankets. Be real. Or be quiet.

Use nouns, facts and the active voice. People remember specifics, chafe at hyperbolic modifiers and at communicators who hide behind the passive voice ("mistakes were made").

Demonstrate. Actions speak more persuasively than words.

Try candor. It's usually unexpected, therefore disarming.

Try truth. It has a ring to it, especially when rivals exaggerate or dissemble.

Know when to quit.

Don't

Use words that are unbelievable. Like "dear friend" at the beginning of a sales pitch.

Use words that are hard to define objectively. Like "quality."

Use adjectives whose aim is to hype. Like "exciting," "wonderful," "super," et. al.

Use unsupported superlatives and comparatives. "Lowest rates in town." "Second to none." Which are heard by skeptical target audiences as "same as everybody else."

Use buzzwords. "World class" and "our people," for example.

Pledge, promise, philosophize. The three Ps. All forgettable and incredible.

Generalize. Ditto.

Use institutional boilerplate. Ditto.

Use public domain music. The aural equivalent of boilerplate, especially in videos.

Be longwinded. Your target audience is as time-constrained and information-laden as you are, so more is less.

Be sloppy. Misspellings, mispronunciations, punctuation and grammatical mistakes, typos, etc. signal your audience that you don't care and/or you're not too swift ("not the sharpest knife in the drawer," says John Madden).

(All-star example: a Michigan trucking company whose rigs carry the slogan, "Commited to quality.")

Bore.

Brag. It's incredibly boring.

Use with care.

Tempering adverbs. "Briefly," "very," "really," "virtually," "significantly," et. al. They're sometimes necessary, sometimes helpful, always tricky.

Special emphases. Underlining, exclamation points, all caps, italics. May be experienced as hype by your skeptical target audience. How to tell? Empathize.

Recommended Resources for Managers

Mail orders to:

Lakewood Books
50 S. Ninth Street
Minneapolis, MN 55402
(800) 707-7769 or (612) 333-0471

Or fax your order to (612) 340-4819

Quantity	Title	$ Amount
_____	50+ Activities to Teach Negotiation *By Ira G. Asherman, $99.95*	_____
_____	Changing Pace; Outdoor Games for Experiential Learning *By Carmine M. Consalvo, $34.95*	_____
_____	The New Training Library *Set of 12 Books, $199.95*	_____
_____	The Best of Creative Training Techniques™ Newsletter *6-pack of 101 Books, By Bob Pike, $69.95*	_____
_____	TRAINING Magazine *12 issues/yr. $78 US, $88 Canada, $99 Other Int'l*	_____
_____	Creative Training Techniques newsletter *12 issues/yr. $99 US, $109 Canada, $119 Other Int'l*	_____
_____	Training Directors' Forum newsletter *12 issues/yr. $118 US, $128 Canada, $138 Other Int'l*	_____
_____	The Lakewood Report on Technology for Learning newsletter *12 issues/yr. $195 US, $205 Canada, $215 Other Int'l*	_____

Subtotal: _____

In Canada add 7% GST #123705485 (applies to all products)   Add GST: _____

In MN add 7% sales tax (does not apply to newsletters)   Add Tax: _____

Shipping and Handling (see chart)   Add Shipping and Handling† _____

Order Total	S & H in U.S.*
Under $25	$6.50
$25.01 - $50.00	$7.50
$50.01 - $100.00	$10.00
$100.01 - $200.00	$12.00
$200.01 - $300.00	$15.00
$300.01 - $500.00	$20.00
Over $500.00	$25.00

*In Canada: Add an additional $5.00
 Other Int'l: Add an additional $15.00
 (via surface mail)
† No S & H on magazines or newsletters

Total Amount: _____

☐ Check or money order is enclosed. Check payable to Lakewood Publications (US funds on a US Bank)

☐ Please Charge: ☐ VISA   ☐ Mastercard   ☐ American Express   ☐ Discover

Card # _____ Exp. ___/___ Signature _____
(required for credit card use)

Name _____ Title _____

Company _____

Address (No PO Boxes) _____

City/State/Zip _____

Country _____

Phone (___) _____ Fax (___) _____